An Elizabethan Adventurer

An Elizabethan Adventurer

The Remarkable Life of Sir Anthony Sherley

Dan O'Sullivan

First published in Great Britain in 2021 by
PEN AND SWORD HISTORY
An imprint of
Pen & Sword Books Ltd
Yorkshire – Philadelphia

Copyright © Dan O'Sullivan, 2021

ISBN 978 1 39900 742 9

The right of Dan O'Sullivan to be identified as Author of this work has been asserted by him in accordance with the Copyright, Designs and Patents Act 1988.

A CIP catalogue record for this book is available from the British Library.

All rights reserved. No part of this book may be reproduced or transmitted in any form or by any means, electronic or mechanical including photocopying, recording or by any information storage and retrieval system, without permission from the Publisher in writing.

Typeset in Times New Roman 11.5/14 by
SJmagic DESIGN SERVICES, India.
Printed and bound by CPI Group (UK) Ltd, Croydon, CR0 4YY

Pen & Sword Books Limited incorporates the imprints of Atlas, Archaeology, Aviation, Discovery, Family History, Fiction, History, Maritime, Military, Military Classics, Politics, Select, Transport, True Crime, Air World, Frontline Publishing, Leo Cooper, Remember When, Seaforth Publishing, The Praetorian Press, Wharncliffe Local History, Wharncliffe Transport, Wharncliffe True Crime and White Owl.

For a complete list of Pen & Sword titles please contact
PEN & SWORD BOOKS LIMITED
47 Church Street, Barnsley, South Yorkshire, S70 2AS, England
E-mail: enquiries@pen-and-sword.co.uk
Website: www.pen-and-sword.co.uk

Or

PEN AND SWORD BOOKS
1950 Lawrence Rd, Havertown, PA 19083, USA
E-mail: Uspen-and-sword@casematepublishers.com
Website: www.penandswordbooks.com

Contents

Map		vi
Introduction		viii
Chapter 1	Sir Thomas senior	1
Chapter 2	The brothers at war	9
Chapter 3	A privateer	16
Chapter 4	To Venice	23
Chapter 5	Sir Thomas Sherley the younger	31
Chapter 6	The journey to Qazvīn	39
Chapter 7	Persia before Abbas	48
Chapter 8	The young Shah	56
Chapter 9	The nature of Shah Abbas	64
Chapter 10	A meeting	73
Chapter 11	Travelling as an ambassador	82
Chapter 12	Opinion at home	91
Chapter 13	Essex and honour	101
Chapter 14	Spying – a downward trajectory	109
Chapter 15	Abbas the Great	119
Chapter 16	Robert Sherley	127
Chapter 17	*Peso Politico*	137
Conclusion		146
Appendix I	Doubtful stories associated with the Sherleys	149
Appendix II	Five authors	152
Appendix III	The uncertainty of letters	155
Appendix IV	A portrait of Anthony Sherley?	156
Endnotes		158

The Travels of Sir Anthony Sherley between 1598 and 1606

Key to Journeys

1st journey: ———— London to Isfahan, 1598-1599

2nd journey: – – – – Isfahan to Rome, 1599-1601

3rd journey: –·–·– Venice to Marrakesh, 1605-1606

Map drawn by David W. Taylor, Great Ayton

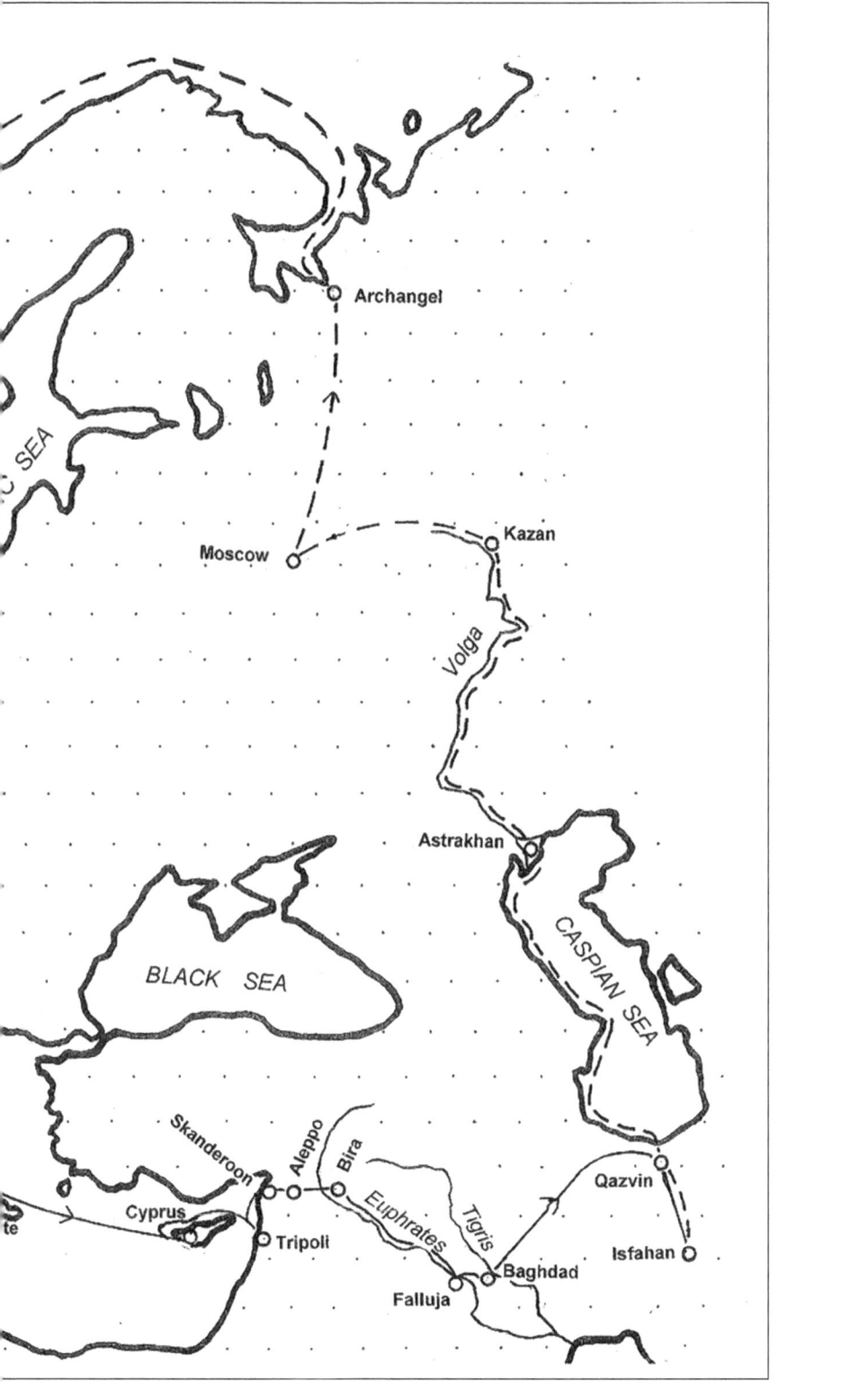

Introduction

I protest unto you I am exceeding faynt. For that unsene thing called honour is so howerly before the eyes of my mynde in so many feares of being taynted by some or other desease, that by Jesue I am farre worst then a meane Commander, he being holpen with his extreame resolution, and I devyded from myself by not knowing what to determyne uppon.

Sir Anthony Sherley[1]

In the sixteenth century there appears to be an increased self-consciousness about the fashioning of human identity as a manipulable, artful process ... a distinctive personality, a characteristic address to the world, a consistent mode of perceiving and behaving.

Stephen Greenblatt[2]

At present the government of the Persians is a monarchy – despotic and absolute, since it is entirely in the hands of a single man who is the sovereign chief both in spiritual as well as in worldly affairs, the complete master of the life and goods of his subjects.

Jean Chardin[3]

The main topic of this book is the life of Sir Anthony Sherley[4] (1565-1633), whom a French historian describes as 'cet étrange et bizarre personnage ... exemple parfait de l'extraordinaire versatilité des hommes de son temps.'[5] I first encountered Sir Anthony when I was researching a book about Sir Thomas Chaloner, the English ambassador to Spain, and his family.[6] The ambassador's son, another Thomas Chaloner, met Sir Anthony in Venice in 1598 when both of them were in the pay of the Earl of Essex (see Chapter 4). Chaloner was impressed by

Introduction

Sherley, so I made a mental resolution to investigate the Sherley family further one day, and this book is the result.

The high point of Sir Anthony's undoubtedly versatile career came in 1598 when he led a group of young gentlemen adventurers on a precarious journey to Persia, a country then relatively unknown in the West. There he met and befriended Shah Abbas, 'the ruthless King who became an Iranian legend,'[7] and was created ambassador by him. He was sent back home to visit the leading princes of Europe and try to organise an alliance between them and Persia against their mutual enemy, the Ottoman Turkish empire.

To make sense of this sensational encounter between West and East – the adventurer and the autocrat – the book includes several chapters on Persia, and on Shah Abbas the Great in particular. Apart from Cyrus the Great, who ruled two millennia earlier, Abbas is the only King of Persia who has ever been labelled 'Great'. He was a charismatic and ambitious ruler who inherited the throne at the age of seventeen in exceptionally difficult conditions, and ruled for over forty years. I include also separate chapters on Anthony's two brothers, whose experiences abroad were almost as striking, though even less successful, than his own. Thomas, a year older than Anthony, was an incompetent privateer who spent nearly three years as a prisoner of the Turks. Robert, some sixteen years younger, was only seventeen when he joined his brother Anthony on the expedition to Persia. When the Shah dispatched Anthony to the courts of Europe, Robert stayed behind, an unofficial hostage against Anthony's guaranteed return. After Anthony failed to return, Abbas sent Robert off to Europe on a similar mission.

After his meeting with the Shah and his elevation to Persian ambassador, things for Anthony started to go very wrong, although this was mainly due to matters far beyond his control. My original title for this book was 'The Rise and Fall of an Elizabethan Adventurer', because Anthony's career could be shown on a graph as a two-dimensional pyramid, rising to a high place, and followed by an irregular but pronounced decline. One of his biographers, Boies Penrose, indicates his awareness of this rise and fall while giving no particular reasons for it. Instead, he makes it sound as if Anthony was subject to some kind of mental decline. He writes, 'His bad qualities developed with age … from 1600 onward his character seemed to change rapidly for the worse.'[8] Without disagreeing with this, or saying that I think Anthony was ever a particularly admirable character, I have tried to provide some explanation as to why the decline started (see chapters 11 and 14): it was the moment when he lost the status of an ambassador and was forced to refashion himself as a cunning 'intelligencer' or spy in the multinational and dangerous world of Venice.

To vary the narrative, I have included a couple of chapters on how the three Sherley brothers were seen at home, and on the cult of honour which motivated Anthony. But to start the ball rolling, my first chapter mainly concerns old Sir Thomas, father of three adventurous sons.

Chapter 1

Sir Thomas senior

On New Year's day 1598, a group of young gentlemen adventurers with their servants set sail from Southwold for the Netherlands. Most of them had recently fought against the Spanish in Brittany under Robert Devereux, Earl of Essex and Queen Elizabeth's favourite courtier. The leader of this little group was Sir Anthony Sherley. The plan, conceived and paid for by Essex, was for them to travel to Ferrara in northern Italy in order to help Cesare d'Este, son of the recently deceased duke, who was trying to assert his claim to the dukedom against Papal and Spanish opposition. Essex at this time was beginning to see his dominant position at Elizabeth's court under threat from his rivals, and the Ferrara project – so typical of Essex – was designed to re-establish his prestige, as well as strike a blow against Spain, the common enemy of Protestant Europe.

Anthony Sherley was at this moment thirty-two years old.[1] He had spent the previous ten years mainly abroad, fighting in France and Holland and then leading an expedition to the Spanish New World in search of glory and plunder. He was a follower and admirer of Essex, and was anxious for further adventures. He had little to keep him in England and wanted to escape from an unhappy marriage that he had contracted two years earlier, probably because his bride happened to be Essex's cousin. Also, he badly needed money since his father was bankrupt and had just been released from prison, his estates having been sequestered by the government.

The trouble was that the Ferrara affair, having been devised by Essex personally, did not have official sanction, and therefore Sherley was leaving the country without the Queen's approval, something that was to cause him major difficulties in the future. In fact, for the rest of his life he never set foot on English soil again.

*****

The Sherleys were of ancient gentry stock with roots going back to the Norman conquest and even beyond.² By the sixteenth century the family had branches in several counties. Anthony's father, Sir Thomas, was married to Anne, daughter of Sir Thomas Kempe of Rye, Kent, and they had three sons and six daughters. The six girls 'married well', as they say, two of them to noblemen, but history relates little about their lives. The three Sherley brothers, Thomas, Anthony and Robert, on the other hand, all embarked on unusual and dangerous careers, leading to national and even international fame, but very little wealth.

Their father, old Sir Thomas, was born in 1542, and until he was in his early forties he led the life of a distinguished and successful county gentleman. His home was Wiston, an attractive house in West Sussex, on the edge of the South Downs. Although much altered, the house still survives, and is today leased by the Foreign Office, which hires it out for meetings and residential conferences. Sir Thomas also owned considerable land and property, not only in Sussex but in several other counties. In particular he owned much of the village of Steyning, not far from Wiston. Steyning was a pocket borough controlled by the Sherleys, which Sir Thomas represented in Parliament for many years. He was also a magistrate, a deputy lieutenant of Sussex and a sheriff of that county. He was gregarious, and known for spending his money freely, for instance expanding Wiston at great expense, converting it into a massive, rambling house, even bigger than it is today, where he could entertain friends, neighbours and officials from London. In a collection of inventories of Wiston there are items which indicate the capacity of the house and the numbers that could be entertained there. These inventories record goods and furniture temporarily seized for debt in 1588, at a time when Sir Thomas had clearly overspent his income. For example:

> lxxi feather beds and lxxii boulsters
> lx paire of sheets
> lxx paire of blankets
> xxx stools of Turkey work and needle work
> lxx pieces of arras hanging.³

It is possible that Sir Thomas had been a Roman Catholic when he was young, before and during the reign of Queen Mary, but if so he certainly turned to the Church of England when Elizabeth became Queen. His cousin and namesake, Sir Thomas Sherley of Bottlebridge, Huntingdonshire, who was himself Catholic, attributed our Sir Thomas's later troubles to the fact that he had deserted the ancient faith of his fathers.[4] Certainly, when he was sheriff of Sussex he had duties concerned with investigating disloyal Catholics, duties which he would never have been entrusted with had there been any suspicion that he himself was inclined to Catholicism. For instance, he was ordered to hold Anne Howard, Countess of Arundel, prisoner for a year at Wiston after she attracted Queen Elizabeth's hostility by becoming a Catholic. This unfortunate lady, aged twenty-five, was pregnant when she was first arrested, and she gave birth to her first child, Elizabeth, at Wiston, while her husband, Philip, Duke of Arundel, who had also converted to Rome, was a prisoner in the Tower of London. When the baby was born she was baptised a Protestant against her mother's wishes.

It was Sir Thomas's duty to question Anne about who had converted her, how many masses she had attended, and whether she had ever hidden priests at Arundel castle. But she was a strong-minded woman who gave away very little: 'She denies speaking ill, or indeed at all, about Elizabeth's government, denies having held conference with any seminary or Jesuit priest, denies having heard Mass, been shriven. or reconciled, and denies knowledge of, or assistance to, those "evil affected" toward the state's religion and wishing to leave the realm.'[5] Sir Thomas's questions and Anne Howard's replies are among the Domestic State Papers at Kew.[6]

One other notable fact about Sir Thomas Sherley was that he was close to that influential courtier and favourite of Elizabeth, Robert Dudley, 1st Earl of Leicester. It is in fact likely that it was Leicester who had earlier picked Sir Thomas to be sheriff of Sussex. In 1585 Leicester was making plans to lead an English army to the Netherlands to help the Dutch rebels in their long struggle for independence against Spain. An experienced Spanish general, Alexander Farnese, Duke of Parma, was threatening to occupy the entire country, including channel ports such as Flushing and Brielle, after which he would be in a position to organise an invasion of England. Queen Elizabeth had watched events in the Netherlands with increasing anxiety, especially after the assassination of the Dutch leader, William of Orange in 1584, followed by the fall of Antwerp to the Spanish the following year.

Leicester and his allies at court demanded that he be sent in command of an English army to help the Dutch, but the Queen still hesitated because she hated having to spend large sums of money, and was always reluctant to assist rebels. Also, she was loath to be parted from Leicester and allow him to travel abroad, especially as he was getting on in years and not particularly fit. But these factors were outweighed by the threat posed by Parma. Therefore, after much hesitation Leicester was finally given his orders, and he hurried to obey them before Elizabeth changed her mind. A force was recruited, and Sir Thomas and his two elder sons, Thomas and Anthony, were to be part of it.

At this moment, due to Sir Thomas's spendthrift habits, the family were probably starting to experience financial problems, which they may have hoped to solve during the campaign. All three Sherleys were made captains of companies, although this was a mere formality in their father's case since he was also part of the commander-in-chief's personal staff. A company usually comprised about a hundred men, whether cavalry or foot soldiers. It is remarkable how many young gentlemen like the Sherley brothers, with the right connections but totally lacking military experience, were made company commanders. This was mainly an army of amateurs – and it was to show.

The English arrived at Flushing in December 1585, to an unparalleled reception of booming guns, a flotilla of welcoming boats, and torchlight processions in honour of Leicester, almost as if he were about to be crowned king. The earl clearly enjoyed playing his part in the celebrations, but those who knew him well had their misgivings. He was fifty-four years old, bulky and corpulent, with a ruddy complexion probably connected with the severe stomach pains he sometimes suffered from. Many wondered how he would cope with the stresses and challenges awaiting him.

Over the next three weeks Leicester's personal retinue made a triumphal progress through the Netherlands, or rather that part of it not yet occupied by the Spanish. Each town tried to outdo its neighbours in displays of patriotism and enthusiasm for England. In these welcoming displays, Leicester figured as a Hercules, a Moses freeing the Israelites from Egypt, a Joshua leading his people into battle. It was clear the Dutch did not see him as just a military general but as their saviour, ready to take on the role of leadership over the entire nation. There was one especially lavish banquet at Delft on Christmas Eve. Pigs were served on their feet, pheasants in their feathers, baked swans with their necks thrust through gigantic pie crusts. Unfortunately, this was one of several occasions when the young gallants of Leicester's retinue behaved badly, causing offence to their respectable hosts. It seemed that only one long table had been provided for the English guests so they rushed across to grab seats meant for their Dutch hosts, with violent disputes and a smashing of glassware as they came.[7]

Their travels ended at The Hague where the commander-in-chief set up his headquarters, and where Sir Thomas Sherley and other senior officers remained while most of the English forces were sent off to garrison various Dutch towns. Leicester, who had enjoyed all the adulation, now faced the difficult task of planning his precise role, which involved, as well as fighting the Spanish, building a working relationship with his allies.

This was where he made his first, and greatest, mistake. When a delegation from the Dutch States General, or Parliament, visited his house they offered him the supreme governorship of the Netherlands, and he was so flattered that he accepted. 'They have given him the absolute authority to govern, which surely was their wisest course,' wrote Sherley to Walsingham in London.[8] However, Elizabeth did not agree and flew into a rage when she heard the news. She had specifically warned Leicester against accepting such authority because she still hoped that an agreement between Spain and England might be worked out, and this made it far less likely. Leicester now sent his old friend, Sir Thomas Sherley, to try and placate the Queen, but for a long time she refused either to see him or to read the letter he brought her from Leicester. After some weeks she partially relented, and when Sherley told her Leicester was ill, agreed to send her personal doctor to look after him.

Shortly afterwards, Leicester appointed Sherley to be Treasurer at War, which meant he was to be in charge of the funds sent out from London to pay the soldiers' wages and expenses. We now discover a side of Sir Thomas which had not been apparent when he was a mere country gentleman in Sussex. He turned out to be highly skilled at ways of using his position to make money for himself. To start with, as a company commander he could enjoy the usual income flowing from what were known as dead pays, meaning that he could claim wages for men who were not actually there, perhaps because they had been killed, taken prisoner, or wounded and sent back home. But as treasurer of the whole army, who dealt with the Dutch merchants contracted to supply food and equipment, he had additional opportunities, not open to a mere company captain, to enrich himself. These he quickly learnt to take advantage of, and his income rose steadily.

All this, of course, did not go unnoticed, When Leicester took a six-month break from his duties as commander-in-chief and went back to England, his replacement, Lord Willoughby, made it his business to put the spotlight on what Sherley was up to. The historian David Davies summarises what was discovered:

> Willoughby drew up for Burghley an estimate of what he thought Sherley might be making. First there were his legitimate emoluments, his entertainment or pay, and the one per cent he received from the Queen on all funds he disbursed, plus the one per cent he exacted from all soldiers for having disbursed the funds to them. These sources, thought Willoughby, amounted to £4,120 per year. In addition, he had the money he could embezzle, to use a crude word, in the time-honoured and respectable way as a captain of an infantry company [i.e. dead pays] which, in Sherley's case, could be augmented by what he could get out of the companies commanded by his sons. Then there were the gratuities from grateful officers who were paid before their pay was due, and tokens of gratitude from [Dutch] victualers who were paid before their fellow victualers. Sherley could also pick up a few pounds by buying up from merchants the debts owed them by captains and soldiers. Whereas merchants might despair of collecting, for Sherley it was an easy matter. He stopped the debts out of the soldiers' pay. He also bought up soldiers' claims to back pay, for whereas soldiers might give up hope of being paid it was a simple matter for the paymaster to pay to himself the full amount due the soldier. By no means to be discounted was the money to be made by loaning the Queen's fund at interest. Putting these various devices together, Willoughby believed that Sherley was making £20,000 per annum, or nearly a fifth of the amount necessary to maintain the English forces in the Netherlands for a year.[9]

Sir Thomas senior

In spite of such investigations, Sherley remained Treasurer at War, and in fact for the last few years of his ten-year treasurership his duties increased, because he also became responsible for supplying Elizabeth's forces fighting the Spanish in France, as well as on sea expeditions against Spain and Spanish America. Consequently, he involved himself with a group of London merchants who undertook to supply food to the troops. But due to a series of droughts and bad harvests throughout Europe the prices of grain and meat shot up, which led to the leader of these merchants, William Beecher, becoming bankrupt, and this in turn led to a full scale investigation by the Privy Council into Sherley's dubious dealings and debts. A contemporary, Rowland Whyte, wrote about Sir Thomas, 'he owed the Queen more than he was worth ... his own doings hath undone him. I was told by one of good acount his living rack-rent is but £1,000 a year. He had good friends but now by his own indiscretion he hath in sort lost them.'[10]

As a result, in 1597 all Sherley's lands and property were confiscated until he could pay back what he was said to owe the Queen, and he was committed to prison. He told Robert Cecil, Elizabeth's new Secretary of State, that he could hardly arrange to repay his debts from prison. This, he complained, was 'a strange and most extraordinary course of handling, and such as I never heard to be offered to any man in this world, which is that before any accounts be determined, or any certain debts known upon me, I should make over all my lands ... to be returned to me when the Queen's Majesty is satisfied; and in the meantime no provision of livelihood for me, my wife, and children.'[11] As a result he was given leave to attend to his affairs during the day, provided he returned to prison at night.

On 15 March 1604, he was again in trouble. Elected MP for Steyning, he was riding through London with King James prior to the opening of Parliament a few days later when he was arrested for debt by a City goldsmith and taken to the Fleet. This raised the whole question of the privilege of freedom from arrest for MPs, and after several weeks of parliamentary activity, a special bill was passed in haste through both Houses. Sherley was released and triumphantly took his seat. The final form of this law was fixed in 1604 and is known as Shirley's case.[12]

That same year Sir Thomas allegedly offered the new king, James I, advice on how to raise extra funds by creating a class of hereditary knights called baronets. Evidence for this comes from a statement by

Sir Thomas's eldest son, Sir Thomas, who wrote to the king after his father's death: 'My Father (being a man of most excellent and working wit), did find out the device for the making of Baronets, which brought to your Majesty's coffers well nigh a hundred thousand pounds for which he was promised good recompence which he never had.'[13]

Sir Thomas's remaining years were sad ones, as he struggled to retain Wiston and his other estates in the face of crushing debt. We leave him with this comment from a distant descendant, the nineteenth century historian Evelyn Shirley: 'His long, but unfortunate life was perhaps in some measure the cause of the erratick career, and romantick adventures of his three knightly sons.'

Sir Thomas was buried near Wiston, and a grand monument to him and his wife, Anne, was set up on the eastern wall of St Mary's Church next to Wiston House. This included effigies of the couple, together with a black marble obituary tablet. The monument was badly damaged in the civil war, although fragments from it are still kept in the granary above the Wiston stables. The obituary states:

> HERE LYETH Y^E BODY OF S^R THOMAS SHIRLEY
> KNIGHT WHO DECEASED IN OCTOBER 1612 WHO
> MARYED VUTO M^S ANNE KEMPE DAUGHTER OF
> SIR THOMAS KEMPE KNIGHT, WITH WHOM HE
> LIVED IN WEDLOCK Y^E SPACE OF LIII YEARS.
> BY WHOM HE HAD 12 CHIL-DREN 5 SONNES &
> 7 DAVGHTERS THREE OF WHOM DYED IN THEIR
> INFANCYES THE RESIDVE BEINGE 3 SONNES
> & DAUGHTERS LYVED TO BE MARYED AS IS
> EX-PRESSED VPON THIS MONYMENT[14]

Chapter 2

The brothers at war

Having taken the story of old Sir Thomas up to his incarceration in the Fleet prison and subsequent decline, it is now time to catch up with his two older sons. In 1585 Anthony and Thomas accompanied their father to the Netherlands, where the Spanish seemed to be capturing one town after another. Since few had any experience of war, the English troops were amateurish and inexperienced, especially compared with the battle-hardened Spanish. They were also badly equipped and not always paid regularly. This was largely due to issues of corruption, as discussed in the previous chapter. Elizabeth sent over large amounts of money which tended to become reduced as it made its way down the military hierarchy until it reached the ordinary soldiers, by which time much of it had disappeared. Numbers of England's young noblemen and gentry had joined the army looking forward to adventures that could not be experienced in peacetime, and many of them expected to be made the captain of a company, a rank which promised opportunities to make a profit out of war. As mentioned above, a company, whether of infantry or cavalry, theoretically consisted of a hundred men, though in practice the number was often far less. Thomas, who was twenty-one, and Anthony, a year younger, both became captains, most likely owing to the close friendship between their father and Leicester.

After the welcome celebrations had finished, many companies were dispatched to various parts of the Netherlands to garrison cities that might come under enemy attack. They were not always welcomed, partly because their presence entailed additional expense for the citizens. Anthony went to Brielle, a port in the southern Netherlands, where he struggled to control a company that turned out to be exceedingly undisciplined, quarrelling with the citizens, and raiding neighbouring farms to supplement their rations. They behaved rather better after four of them had been executed by order of the commander of that province, Lord Burgh.

Anthony's brother was even less fortunate. When his cavalry company reached Zwolle, the town in the north which they were supposed to garrison, they were refused entry on the grounds that there already was an adequate garrison, so the soldiers and their horses had to spend the night outside the town walls, relaxing, eating and copiously drinking what the town council generously provided for them. At this point Thomas Sherley was absent, possibly visiting England, and his lieutenant had ridden off to inform his superiors of the problem. In the small hours a Spanish force, whom nobody had suspected were in the vicinity, launched a surprise attack, killing or wounding nearly half the company. After the subsequent investigation, Thomas was dismissed from the army and sent back home in disgrace. However, within a few months he was apparently forgiven, and posted to Ireland, where it seems he distinguished himself fighting against Irish rebels and receiving a knighthood from the Lord Deputy, Sir William Fitzwilliam. Meanwhile, Anthony's company had been sent back to England to join in a voyage planned against Spain and Portugal. He was chosen to take over his brother's company, and found himself in charge of horsemen instead of foot soldiers.

Before this appointment, Anthony had, it is said, displayed great courage in what turned out to be the most famous event of the entire campaign, the battle, or rather skirmish, outside Zutphen.[1] This city was situated on the main route that Parma had to take to reach the Dutch ports and was held by the Spanish, but it had been under siege for several weeks and the inhabitants were running out of supplies. Spies had informed Leicester that a wagon train bringing food was on its way to the city. Unfortunately, the English had greatly underestimated the strength of the wagon train's escort, and only about 500 men had been selected for the ambush. However, a small group of English cavalry – including some of the most prestigious young noblemen and gentry in the army, many of whom were no doubt tired of uneventful garrison duties – had decided, without their commander-in-chief's permission, to join in the ambush that Leicester was planning against the wagons. Anthony Sherley was one of the group, and so was the youth who was to be his future patron, Walter Devereux, Earl of Essex. Both were aged twenty-one.

The Victorian historian J. L. Motley takes up the story. He tells us that by 5.00 am that morning the group were in place. There was a thick fog and they could hardly see ten yards ahead. Eventually they heard from far off the measured tramp of soldiers and the creaking of wagon wheels. Suddenly the fog rolled away like a curtain and they found themselves face to face with a force of some 3,000 men, with their cavalry out in front. This consisted of several hundred Spanish, Italian and Albanian horsemen. Behind were the lumbering wagons guarded by musketeers and pikemen on each side of the wide track. There was no time to consider possible retreat. Essex shouted, 'Follow me, good lads, for the honour of England and England's Queen,' and as he spoke he dashed into the enemy cavalry, overthrew the first horse and rider, shivered his own spear to splinters, and then, swinging his axe, dashed merrily forward. The whole little band, compact as an arrow head, flew after him, pierced clean through the Spanish cavalry and on to the wagons. Only when they came up against concentrated fire from the musketeers were they forced to wheel, retreat, and then attack again. Time and again they charged, scattering the enemy horse in all directions, only to retreat from a hail of musket balls when they reached the wagons.[2]

In spite of all this bravado, the Spanish forces won the day, and the wagon train was able to reach the gates of Zutphen and relieve its garrison. Of course, this skirmish is most famous for the death of Leicester's nephew, the gifted and dashing Sir Philip Sidney, who was wounded in the thigh by a musket ball and died of gangrene a month later. But as far as our story is concerned Zutphen is important as the first time Anthony Sherley had seen Essex in action, and most likely the moment when, inspired by such romantic bravery, he made the decision to throw in his lot with him.

By this time Essex had become a favourite of the Queen, having first been introduced to court by his uncle, Leicester. His courage in battle, and his noble lineage was to attract the devotion of young gentlemen throughout the kingdom. They looked to him for leadership and wanted to share in his 'culture of honour'. These gallants believed that honour was actually the only thing in the world worth living, or even dying, for: not fortune or family, but one's personal honour, which was, of course, tied up with one's devotion to queen and country. This was, in their eyes the supreme virtue.

Anthony's future devotion to Essex is confirmed in his account of his travels, published many years later. He wrote that as a young man he looked for virtuous examples to follow, 'Amongst which was the ever-living in honour earl of Essex ... so I desired to make him the patterne of my civill life, and from him to draw a worthy modell of all my actions.'[3] Much of his behaviour, as described in the next few chapters, seems to confirm this ambition, until the fall of his patron turned out to be the turning point of his entire career.

In another book, written towards the end of his life, Sherley recounts in detail an event that apparently took place at the beginning of 1586, or early the following year, and in which he claimed to have played a major role.[4] His story is that Leicester entrusted him with a vital secret mission, which was to take two letters to the Spanish commander, the Duke of Parma, and deliver them personally. One of the letters purported to be from Mary, Queen of Scots, then a prisoner in Fotheringhay Castle, but it had actually been forged by her secretary, Claude Nau. In it Mary proposed marriage to the duke, and then suggested that together they could seize the throne of England. The other letter was from Leicester allegedly supporting the project. Anthony claimed that he made his way to Bruges, met Parma, and delivered the letters. He also claimed that it was Parma's uncertainty over what to do about these proposals, which he believed were genuine, that led him to deliberately hesitate before obeying the King of Spain's instructions to march his forces north to meet up with the Armada the following year. It has to be said that the entire story seems highly improbable, given Anthony's youth at the time, and also the lack of any corroborating evidence in contemporary records. Furthermore, the timing of Mary's execution (in February 1587) seems to call into question the existence of this whole plot.[5]

In early 1588 Leicester gave up his post as commander-in-chief in the Netherlands, and retired home exhausted, to die within the year. By now the focus of anti-Spanish activity had shifted to France, where a new king, the Protestant Henry IV, found his throne threatened by a combination of the French Catholic League and their ally, Spain. Elizabeth now agreed to send a force to aid Henry. Anthony Sherley as a member of that force, which was commanded by Lord Willoughby, took part in a three-month campaign in which he is said to have distinguished himself, though details are lacking.

Within months of his return home he was involved in yet another campaign, this time in Brittany where Spanish troops had landed at

Saint-Nazaire, threatening to open a new front against the beleaguered French king. Elizabeth was determined to prevent this, and in 1591 an army was dispatched under Sir John Norris. This time Sherley held a superior position as commander of one of the three regiments involved. Though the campaign itself was indecisive, he again played an important role in a battle near Châtelaudren where a Spanish force of some 500 horse and 6,000 foot descended upon the English. Sherley led the English cavalry against the attackers, personally killing a Spanish captain, and was credited with single-handedly turning the tide of battle. The next day, with a force of only fifteen horse, he repulsed a Spanish counter-attack, though his own horse was shot from under him.[6]

In 1593 Anthony Sherley was summoned by Henry IV to his court in order to receive a knighthood. This was the same year that the French king converted to the Catholic faith, uttering his famous saying, 'Paris is well worth a mass'. Sherley was created knight of the order of St Michael as a reward for his military services to France. This particular decoration came fairly low in the pecking order, having been conferred on so many that it was known in France as 'the dog collar to fit all dogs'.[7] Nevertheless, as a badge of honour and status it meant a great deal to Sherley, as subsequent events showed. Essex, his patron, was now starting to create large numbers of knights whenever his position as commander-in-chief, by sea or land, allowed. Those knighted by him considered themselves honour-bound to follow their leader through thick and thin, much as in former times the tenants and retainers of a great feudal lord would follow their leader into battle. Sherley had not received his knighthood from Essex personally, but from Henry IV, the Earl's friend and ally, which was perhaps the next best thing. Now he was truly a member of that noble Essexian band.

When the Queen heard about Sherley's knighthood she was very angry, and it is on this occasion that she is supposed to have remarked, 'I will not have my sheep marked with a strange brand, nor suffer them to follow the pipe of a strange shepherd.'[8] The French king had converted to Rome in order to end the civil war in France, and Elizabeth suspected that the oath Sherley had taken during his knighthood ceremony might have committed him to supporting a Catholic monarch. Sherley was imprisoned and questioned about this oath, and whether he had sworn allegiance to Henry, which he denied. He was kept in the Fleet prison for at least a month and then interrogated again, and ordered to disclaim his knighthood. His interrogators reported back to Robert Cecil, that 'he would by no means yield, and notwithstanding our strict urging him in duty thereunto, yet this was his final and resolute answer. That this matter concerned his reputation, more dear to him than his life ... desiring rather to die than live with disgrace.'[9] Eventually a compromise was reached by which the knightly insignia of the order was sent back to France, but from now on Sherley called himself Sir Anthony, and would be referred to as such even in official documents. Honour was satisfied, and he was released from prison to resume his rank of colonel of a regiment in Brittany, where he remained until 1595. There is no indication that during all the period he served in France he was anything other than a brave and dutiful soldier.

At about this time Anthony secretly married Essex's cousin, Frances Vernon, a young lady of the court. Essex's aunt, Elizabeth Devereux, was Frances' mother, having married a Vernon. Thus Sir Anthony was linking himself by blood to the Devereux lineage, and strengthening his status within Essex's community of honour. And Frances Vernon herself had a sister, Elizabeth, who was the mistress of Essex's close friend, the Earl of Southampton, whom she was to marry a few years later. When news about Anthony's marriage came to the Queen's ears, she was angry with him all over again and he was banned from court. He and Frances moved to Inglefield, a property in Berkshire which Essex sold to him.[10] Anthony wrote to Robert Cecil, 'I am here in the country and as far as I can judge exiled from all hope of recovering such grace in the court as my best endeavours have ever held their course for.'[11] Cecil suspected that Anthony's father had organised the match but old Sir Thomas wrote back indignantly denying the charge: 'the marriage was made and concluded by my son himself without my privity. The Earl [of Essex] was the first that brake it unto me when my son was in France and I had no reason to refuse to give my consent.'[12]

Apart from these facts next to nothing is known about Frances, though we can guess that from the start the married couple did not get on. It could not have been long after they set up house together in Inglefield that Anthony started planning a new project – an ambitious voyage of privateering and plunder against Spanish possessions. Once he had set off, the two hardly ever saw each other again. It is true that many years later, when he was living in Spain, there is a brief reference in a Spanish document to his having a young son (see Chapter 17), but as this son's name was Diego it seems very unlikely that his mother was Frances Vernon. There is one half-joking reference to the marriage in a letter written by the gossipy correspondent, Rowland Whyte: 'Sir Anthony Sherley goes forward on his voyage very well furnished, and led by the strange fortune of his marriage to undertake any course that might occupy his mind from thinking on her vainest words.'[13] The implication here is that being able to get away from his wife was one of the motives for Anthony's going off on his voyage, and this is all we know.

Chapter 3

A privateer

On 26 September 1580, after a three years circumnavigation of the world, Drake's *Golden Hind* sailed into Plymouth carrying a rich cargo of captured Spanish treasures. The Queen's half-share of the profits was worth more than the rest of the Crown's income for that entire year, and Drake received a knighthood for his efforts. Inspired by his success, dozens of young men took up privateering (a word that didn't then exist), hoping to make a fortune by capturing Spanish or Portuguese ships on the high seas, or attacking and looting their settlements in the New World or along the African coast. (The same year as Drake's arrival back home, Philip II of Spain had also become king of Portugal.) A few years later, when hostility to Spain had developed into open war, such activities became officially approved, and formal commissions were issued by Elizabeth's Privy Council to would-be privateers. But the difference between licensed privateering against Spanish possessions, and outright piracy on the high seas against all comers was not always very clear to those who participated.

The Victorian historian James Anthony Froude, writing in the heyday of the British empire, was sympathetic to these Elizabethan freebooters. He wrote, 'Piracy would be the very source and seed vessel from which the naval power of England was about to rise.' It was, he alleges, 'the first beginnings of that proud power which has planted the saplings of the English race in every quarter of the globe, has covered the ocean with its merchant fleets, and flaunts its flag in easy supremacy among the nations of the earth.'[1] Today, we might see things a little differently. Piracy was an ugly business even when totally ineffective, as is shown by the activities of people like Anthony, and later Thomas, Sherley.

Sir Anthony (as we must now call him) planned to sail to the Gulf of Guinea and capture the small island of São Tomé which was the depot where the Portuguese stored sugar from West Africa, intended for export to the world. In 1595 Anthony's father bought nine ships for his son, and

A privateer

organised the recruitment of 1,500 soldiers. It is remarkable that old Sir Thomas had the funds and the will to subsidise this risky project, considering that his role as Treasurer at War was at this time becoming increasingly demanding and problematic. But sugar was then a highly prized commodity, and we know that both father and son were always up for a gamble. A successful raid on São Tomé might have paid for the entire project and also made a healthy profit.

One problem facing Sir Anthony was the need to make his expedition legal by obtaining a government certificate that endorsed the plan. This could have been an awkward and expensive quest since many others wanted the same thing. The obvious way to do it was to apply for a 'letter of marque and reprisal' (see Chapter 5), but a cheaper way, he hoped, was to legalise his ships as part of the forthcoming Essex expedition to Spain. Eventually he succeeded, but only by personally applying to the Earl of Essex for a suitable certificate. At this moment Essex and Charles Howard, the Lord Admiral, were planning to lead an expedition to Cádiz in order to destroy the fleet which the Spanish were collecting against England. Therefore the certificate which Essex obtained for Sherley was actually a sub-commission, under cover of helping Essex and Howard prepare their Cádiz project: 'Commission of Lord Admiral Howard and the Earl of Essex. The Lord Generals to Sir Anthony Sherley to levy, muster and arm all volunteers for her Majesty's service to the number of 1,500, and also to be captain and commander of all ships set forth at the charge of himself and Sir Thomas Sherley, Treasurer at War, in this expedition.'[2]

Unfortunately, the nature of this commission meant that when Sherley eventually took his men and ships to Plymouth, where Essex and Howard were mustering their own expedition, he found that he was legally bound to hand over to them part of his own fleet – four ships and 500 soldiers. This left him uncertain whether what he had left was enough for a full-scale attack on São Tomé. Nevertheless, he finally set off in May 1596, a few weeks before Essex's Cádiz venture.[3]

Most of our information about Sherley's naval exploit comes from the report of the voyage printed in Hakluyt's *Voyages*, from which the quotations in the following paragraphs are taken.[4] This anonymous account, presumably by a member of the expedition, is so adulatory of Sherley that it sometimes seems implausible. The squadron, we are told, sailed down the Spanish coast and then the west coast of Africa, looking for prizes, without much success. Off Cape Verde Anthony became ill, along with many others. In fact, he was so ill that he thought he was going to die, so, according to the Hakluyt account, he gathered together the captains from his other ships and made a long speech with many references to their Christian faith, their duty to Queen Elizabeth, and also to his successor if he himself died. 'And because we came for his love into this action, that for his sake we would so love together as if himself were still living with us, and that we would follow as our chief commander him unto whom he would give commission to succeed himself: all which with solemn protestation we granted to obey.' This was slightly ironic in that the whole of the squadron, except the *Beavis*, the ship Sherley himself was on, would ultimately desert him and return home.

Although the commander recovered from his sickness, it was thought better to give up the project, and sail to the West Indies instead, owing to the infectious nature of the coastline as well as the difficulty in approaching São Tomé, with its dangerous shoals. On the way they decided to pillage a suitable town in the Cape Verde Islands, also under Portuguese control, and Praia on St Iago was chosen. It was easily taken, but nothing worth looting was found. 'Being here on shore, and finding nothing left in the town, divers of our company were very importunate with our General that he would go to the city of S. Iago being 6 miles off; through their importunity he yielded consent, and so we marched towards the city with 280 soldiers.' When they got there they could see what a difficult task faced them: 'upon the front of the town the sea beateth, the rest standeth between two mighty cliffs, not accessible but by one small path.' There were three forts, two beside the sea and one looking down on the town from high up on a cliff. The path itself was along a natural trench, so that if they followed it, shot and stones could be rained down on them from both sides. Nevertheless, Sherley 'with an excellent resolution (like unto himself) cryed out: all courage my hearts. The day is ours now, shew your selves as I know you will: and so presently we descended into the trench.'

Along this sunken pathway Sherley's troops gave as good as they got, and reached the town where 'we were received with the streets full of soldiers,' and a struggle took place in which 'their captain and divers of them being slain, fear possessing them, they fled,' and the English captured the town and the two lower forts. However, Sherley knew there would be a counter-attack from the fort on the hill, so in preparation they barricaded all the streets in the town. After six hours the attack came, and during the ensuing battle eighty English were killed or wounded, and 250 of the enemy. 'But they still prosecuted their assault, not giving us time either to sleep or eat, so that we were in exceeding extremity, for their forces did increase to the number of three thousand persons, but we lost of our poor number.' Eventually, Sherley managed to get a message to his ships to sail round to the town, start firing at the upper fort at ten o'clock that night, and send all their boats ashore. This was done, and in the dark the English were able to leave the town and get back to their ships, largely because the Portuguese were misled into thinking they were planning to attack the fort. 'So ended an utterly fruitless enterprise, typically Elizabethan, totally irrational, but redeemed by brilliant courage and high devotion,' writes one commentator, comparing it to the attack near Zutphen, that earlier episode in Sherley's colourful career.[5]

His expedition now sailed to Domenica in the Leeward Islands where they rested for six weeks, bathing in hot springs and shaking off the infections many had caught off the West African coast. After this holiday they proceeded northwards to try their luck at Jamaica, then a relatively neglected part of the Spanish New World. The island was poor and uncultivated, with a small Spanish population ruling over what was left of the indigenous Taino people, by then much decimated by conquest and European diseases. There was only one settlement of any size, Santiago de la Vega (today, Spanish Town), most of whose inhabitants cultivated cassava and were far from well off. Sherley arrived off the Jamaican coast close to where Kingston is today, and marched his forces overland to reach Santiago.

For what happened in Jamaica we have two sources: the Hakluyt account, and also – most unusually – some documents giving us the Spanish point of view.[6] This latter consists of petitions to the Spanish authorities for help after the damage caused by the English. According to Hakluyt, when they reached the town, 'the people all on horseback made shew of great matters, but did nothing. Now being masters of the town and whole isle, the people submitted themselves to our general's mercy: and they provided for us great store of dried beef and cassava meal, a base food yet the best that the country yieldeth ... They were in fine at our general's devotion, to dispose of all things as he pleased, so that now we were as one people & in peace together.'

However, the Spanish petitioners did not exactly share these sentiments. According to them, most of the 160 inhabitants of Santiago de la Vega fled to the surrounding woods on the appearance of the English, who proceeded to loot and burn down a number of houses. They found an Indian guide named Pedro who showed them where the governor of the town was hiding, and from him they demanded a large quantity of meat and cassava – threatening otherwise to destroy the whole place. The governor then held a meeting with other leading citizens, and it was decided, on the advice of the abbot of the local convent, not to give the English what they asked for, 'for having it they could harm ships coming from Spain and other ships of the Indies, and could maintain themselves in these parts if they had food.' This was agreed by the governor, but when Sherley heard about it he was furious. About another sixty houses were burnt down, and a party of soldiers were sent to arrest the abbot, who managed to escape just before they arrived. He fled through the woods to the estate of the town's treasurer, who 'since the said abbot had escaped quite naked, provided him with a jacket and a cloth pair of breeches.'

Finally, the English were given the food demanded, and also horses and carts to transport it to their ships which were anchored several miles away. Sherley's soldiers also quitted the town, leaving it even poorer than when they arrived, and all set off on the next leg of their Caribbean cruise. It was now the beginning of March 1597, and the ships made for the bay of Honduras where they had heard that the town of Trujillo was there for the sacking. But it was too well defended, so they instead attacked Puerto de Cavallos, lower down in the bay. Here 'we presently prevailed,' but this settlement turned out to be 'the most poor and miserable place of all India'. After this disappointment, relates the Hakluyt chronicler, 'our hopes were all frustrate and no likelihood remaining how we could by any means make a voyage: our General, reserving unto himself his silent inward impatience, laboured to do some memorable thing.' This memorable thing was to try and discover a passage through to the Pacific Ocean where, Sherley felt sure, unsuspecting Spanish merchant ships could easily be taken. So he left most of his fleet moored to await his return, and with a few men in small boats set off westward up Lake Izabal in what is now Guatemala. They took with them a larger boat that had been divided into sections so that, if necessary, it could be carried across land and then reassembled. The hope was to find a navigable river that flowed into the Pacific.

A privateer

However, no such river was discovered, many of the men became ill, and they had to return to the ships. Sherley now came up with an even more dubious plan: to take two ships northwards to Newfoundland, revictual and enlist fresh men, return and rejoin the rest of the fleet off Cuba, and then proceed southwards to the Straits of Magellan, enter the Pacific, and return home by circumnavigating the world. Considering that Sherley's men had already been at sea for a year without any prospect of profit, what happened when they heard about this plan was hardly unexpected, although Hakluyt's author seems surprised: 'Being thwart Havana, by what chance I know not, but all his ships forsook him the 13 of May, and here in a desperate place he was left desperately alone … our misery in the Admiral [i.e. the *Beavis*] was very great, for there was not one in the ship that was ever before in the Indies.'

The *Beavis* proceeded northwards to Newfoundland 'not having one hours victuals to spare,' and then, having bought the necessary supplies, sailed for England, arriving at Dover in mid-July. Sherley returned to find his father in prison, bankrupt and removed from his office as Treasurer at War. The need to repair the family fortunes was now even more urgent, and he was just in time to join an ambitious voyage, again commanded by Essex, who had returned from his Cádiz voyage somewhat of a hero. 'Poor Anthony Sherley is come home alive but poor, and goeth out with the Earl,' wrote Robert Cecil to a friend.[7] He was appointed sergeant major, meaning that, under his commander, Essex, he was responsible for the soldiers on board the ships. He was, in other words, one of the superior officers in charge of the fleet. The most prominent leaders, apart from Essex, were Lord Thomas Howard and Sir Walter Raleigh.

Before they all set off, Essex sent Sherley to London to report to Robert Cecil and the Queen about their last minute preparations. It seems from letters between Essex and Cecil that at this point in his career Sherley had been restored to royal favour: 'do him with Her Majesty what favor you can, for, on my credit, he doth wonderfully deserve to be cherished', wrote Essex to Cecil.[8] And Cecil wrote back, 'Sir Anthony Sherley, his instructions and letters were read by the Queen, and he himself presented by my Lord Howard and me, [and] used with great favour both in the privy and [with-]drawing chamber'[9].

The Islands Voyage, as it was later called, was an ambitious project. Over a hundred ships were involved, including transport vessels, sundry privateers, and a squadron of Dutch warships. The main object was to destroy a fleet of Spanish ships that were sheltering in the port of Ferrol and intended for another armada against England. A secondary object was to sail to the Azores and there ambush the treasure fleet which every summer brought silver from America to Spain. Unfortunately, neither of these goals was achieved, largely due to factional disputes and rivalry among the leaders of the expedition. When they reached Ferrol a decision was made not to try and enter the harbour, or even to send in fire ships, as the wind was contrary. Instead, they headed towards the Azores where a major misunderstanding occurred between Raleigh and Essex.

Raleigh had been told by Essex to wait near Fayal in the Azores until he arrived, but having lingered there several days he eventually decided to land. He captured the island, thus achieving a rare success for the expedition, but Essex, when he finally turned up, was very angry and his supporters tried to persuade him to have Raleigh court-marshalled for disobeying orders. This is the only time during the Islands Voyage that the sources mention Sherley, who was clearly a member of the Essex faction, and therefore an enemy of Raleigh: 'All our proceedings in Fayall were by Sir Guillie Merrick, at large related unto our General … and wrested into an evil sense by him [Merrick], Sir Christopher Blount, Sir Anthony Sherley, and others, by putting my Lord [Essex] in the head that these parts were played by the Rear Admiral [Raleigh] only to steal honour and reputation from him … against whom they gave out that he was well worthy to lose his head.'[10] Eventually, Lord Howard persuaded the two leaders to make peace, but, as David Davies points out, if the Merrick group had won the argument, Raleigh would have been beheaded much earlier than he actually was.[11]

Due to a series of misunderstandings and misjudgements by the captains of various ships, the English did not manage to intercept the Spanish treasure ships, and their fleet returned to Plymouth having failed in both its objectives. Meanwhile, the Spanish ships in Ferrol, with nothing to stop them en route, set out to proceed to Falmouth, as planned. It was only their dispersal by powerful storms that prevented a landing on English soil, which might have altered the course of history. The Queen severely criticised Essex for the failure of his mission, and he was never again given charge of a seafaring expedition. Sherley, however, although he had been involved in two unsuccessful voyages, was soon put in charge of another project by his noble patron.

Chapter 4

To Venice

After his return from the Islands Voyage, Essex's new project involved a plunge into the complex maelstrom of Italian politics. His relations with Elizabeth having become rather awkward after his naval failure, Essex needed to achieve something clearly useful for the country but which did not involve the Queen directly. He chose Ferrara where the duke, Alfonso II, had just died and where the succession was in dispute. Alfonso had left the state to his nephew, Cesare d'Este, but Cesare's succession was challenged on the grounds that he was illegitimate. Spain, which already owned Milan as well as Naples, and was therefore closely involved in Italian politics, opposed Cesare's claim, as did the papacy.

Essex was aware that the Spanish were still planning to send another armada to invade England, and he calculated that if Spanish forces became involved in a struggle over the Ferrara succession, this would distract them from any hostilities against England. His project was to dispatch a group of experienced captains to Ferrara with ample funds with which to persuade or bribe leading citizens into support for Cesare. If challenged, the English government could deny any knowledge of the group's activities. Essex also anticipated that Henry IV of France, as well as Ferdinand, Grand Duke of Tuscany, might well join the conflict on the anti-Spanish side. The man he chose to lead this unofficial project was Sir Anthony Sherley, who had been sergeant major of the forces on the recent voyage. Sometime later, when Anthony was in trouble for leaving the country without the Queen's permission, he argued that 'neither did I go without Her Majesty's knowledge, nor in my opinion licence.'[1]

Whether or not Elizabeth was aware that the group was leaving England, there was certainly another person whom Anthony failed to tell, and that was his father. It seems that he had been lent a large sum of money by old Sir Thomas which he was expected to pay back the week he left, but failed to do so, and now he had vanished. This was particularly devastating for Sir Thomas since he had only just been let out of prison in order to allow him to raise money to pay back what he owed the Queen. In the following letter to Robert Cecil he rails bitterly about his son's conduct:

> It may please your Honour, I am driven most against my will to complain to your Honour of the most unnatural or rather cruel dealing of Anthony Sherley towards me: the case is this. There were two jewels of his pawned for his own debt for £551, whereof he did exceedingly urge me to procure means to redeem them promising most faithfully to see the money satisfied again within ten days. I made means for it even of such friends to give me means to live and without whom I have no means to eat. He hath repaid only £120 and upon Monday last he promised to pay the other £431 and bound his promise with an oath upon his salvation. Monday in the evening my man came to him according to his appointment. He told him it was not then ready but did assure him to have it the next morning, being yesterday, and when my man came to the place where he lived, it was told him that he was gone out of the town, and upon better and further enquiry I do understand that he is gone out of the town with purpose to go beyond the seas, but whether with licence of the Queen's Majesty or to what place I do not know, only I know that I am most vilely handled by him.[2]

Sir Thomas now points out that he had already given Anthony funds for his sea-faring expedition which had never been repaid. He wants Cecil to prevent him going abroad:

> He first wounded my estate by his voyage and now hath more undone me, being in the desperate case that I am in, by this cozening of me of the money which I am no ways able to repay where it was promised. He cannot be far gone for he was seen in London after nine of the clock yesterday ... I truly trust that he may be stayed until he make delivery either of the jewels or of the money. This is wickedness to lay affliction upon affliction upon his poor aged parents.[3]

Having crossed the channel to Holland, the group under Sherley was received at Flushing by Sir Robert Sidney, the English governor of the port, who treated them hospitably though he was not put in the picture as to what they intended to do. They then continued on to Germany, travelling southward until they reached Augsburg, not too far from the German border. There they heard the news that Cesare d'Este had made a pact with the Pope so that their services in Ferrara would no longer be required. What with their generous funding by Essex, and their desire for adventure, they were no doubt very reluctant to return to England, so they must have debated as to what to do next.

We know what they decided and where they went, because Sherley and three of his companions kept records. One account was written by William Parry, a member of the group, who states that the party travelled by coach to Augsburg, 'from whence we hired horses to pass the Alps, in respect that it was not passible by coach.' George Manwaring, another member who kept a journal, explains, 'From Augusta [Augsburg] we went to Venice where we did solace ourselves almost three months.'[4] Solace is the right word here because Venice was the shopping capital of Europe and beyond, famous for its luxury and style. As the contemporary English traveller, Thomas Coryate, wrote in his popular travel guide to Europe: 'Truely such is the supendious glory of it, that at my first entrance thereof it did even amaze or rather ravish my senses. For here is the greatest magnificence of architecture to be seene, that any place under the sunne doth yield. Here you may both see all manner of fashions of attire, and heare all the languages of Christendome.'[5]

Venice was where one could encounter strangers from all nations and all faiths, including even Jews and Moslems. England had expelled Jews three centuries earlier, but here they mixed freely with Christians, and even had their own synagogue. Shakespeare's public understood that Venice was the city, unique in Europe, where a Jewish merchant like Shylock could meet and do deals with Christians, and where a black general (Othello) could marry the daughter of a Venetian nobleman. And, according to Coryate, Venetian tolerance extended to questions of personal morality, although no doubt he grossly exaggerated the number of prostitutes: 'There were so many courtesans that it is thought there are of them in the whole city and other adjacent places at the least twenty thousand, whereof many are esteemed so loose that they are said to open their quivers to every arrow ... So infinite are the allurements of the most famous Calypsos that the fame of them hath drawn many to Venice from some of the remotest parts of Christendome, to contemplate their beauties and enjoy their pleasing dalliances.'[6]

Neil Macgregor sums up the attraction that the city held for foreigners, and perhaps especially for Protestants such as the English: 'Venice, then as now, was the city of dreams, a place where the limits of the possible were endlessly extendable. The metropolis of intoxicating potentiality.'[7] One can easily understand how Sherley's companions found it possible to pass three enjoyable months in Venice. It is also obvious that these young gentlemen from England, who apparently had been dispatched by the famous Earl of Essex, and who were busily engaged in spending his money, would soon attract official attention. According to Parry: 'We remained in Venice ten weeks, in which time Sir Anthony went to the Duke thereof [i.e. the Doge], who entertained him with all princely compliment, sending him to his lodging a royal banquet of all kinds of confected sweet-meats and wine in great abundance; which continued a long time. Who likewise commanded that we should have liberty to see anything in the city worthy the sight, which accordingly we saw, to Sir Anthony's no small cost; for in his rewards he was there and elsewhere most royal.'[8]

During these weeks Sherley spent time and energy searching for any new enterprise that might lead to glory and profit for the group and approval from his patron, Essex. He employed his social skills, which were considerable, to form useful contacts with anyone in the Venetian hierarchy or from abroad who might possibly be of assistance. Unfortunately, due to the collapse of the Ferrara affair there were plenty of others, mercenary soldiers or amateur adventurers, on the same search. Also, not everyone who came into contact with Sherley was equally impressed by his charm. There is a letter from an anonymous correspondent, most probably a Frenchman, to his friend in Frankfurt which has ended up among the Cecil Papers. He describes some of Sir Anthony's less attractive characteristics, obvious even at this early stage in his career – his boastfulness, his carelessness with money, and in particular his apparent willingness to work for whomever might subsidise him and his group. The writer must have met him shortly after his arrival in the city, and was unimpressed. He sent his friend a somewhat caustic account of what he had gleaned from their conversations:

> Here one finds a gentleman named Shurley, accompanied by about twenty-five men in his group, and he spends a very large amount, and those in his entourage are for the most part captains and gentlemen When he arrived the rumour went around that he had come to take part in the war at Ferrara, which he found was already over; nevertheless, he has been sustained over here, and is thinking of spending time in this place. He has been in France, and has been captain of the English light cavalry there; still he speaks French very badly. He unceasingly extols the greatness of Spain and even more that of the Pope, and says that he has received great offers from the one and the other, and that (if he finds nothing better elsewhere), he will see what he decides to do. He says that no matter where the support comes from, he would rather wind up ruined than spend less. If he were wise and of good counsel, he would talk less and would be more to be feared. He has married a close relative of Monsieur le Conte d'Essex and says that he is his great favourite, and that he had received eight thousand pounds sterling to make this voyage over here. But since he is a spendthrift who has spent all his means, and those of his father whom he has ruined, and he lives here on what he has borrowed, one cannot believe that he was sent by the said Count.[9]

It seems unlikely at this early stage in Venice that Sherley had got to the end of Essex's £8,000, but it is surely correct that he was a spendthrift who took little account of the value of money. He enjoyed life's pleasures, and was always generous to his friends and servants. When he ran out of funds he knew how to persuade others to lend. Throughout his career these characteristics were often commented on by others.

Finally, Sherley arrived at a project that might possibly fulfil the necessary criteria – profit, adventure, honour and, if possible, Essex's approval. It involved travelling across Turkish territory to the then almost unknown country of Persia, meeting the king of that realm, and persuading him to reduce the stranglehold which the Portuguese had on seaborne trade with the Far East. Instead, the king would be encouraged to develop new trading relations with other European states including Venice and the up-and-coming northern powers, England and Holland.

This was clearly an undertaking much in the interests of Venice, whose trade with the East had suffered ever since the Portuguese admiral, Albuquerque, had seized the island of Hormuz at the entrance to the Persian Gulf in 1515, turning it into a wealthy and well-defended trading centre. Persian merchants were thereafter allowed to trade via Hormuz provided they paid their dues, and an uneasy but relatively peaceful relationship subsisted between Persia and the Portuguese. It was this relationship that Sherley hoped somehow to upset. He would have been aware that his patron had himself recently developed an interest in furthering a possible trade between England and the East Indies, with its pepper, cloves and other luxury goods. Essex had invested in the very first Dutch voyage to be dispatched to the East via the Cape of Good Hope, and had persuaded an English navigator, John Davis, to join that voyage, which set out in April 1598 – about the same time that Sherley himself arrived in Venice.[10]

According to George Manwaring, Sherley's plan was hatched when he happened to meet the man who was to be his interpreter on his eastern journey:

> It was his fortune to hear of a great traveller, newly come to Venice from the Sophi's [i.e. the Shah of Persia's] court, whose name was Angelo, born in Turkey but a good Christian, who had travelled sixteen years and did speak twenty-four kind of languages. This Angelo did acquaint Sir Anthony of the worthiness of the King of Persia, that he was a gallant soldier, very bountiful and liberal to strangers, and what entertainment he had at his court; assuring Sir Anthony that, if he would go thither, it would be greatly for his advancement; and moreover that he [Angelo] would be his guide, and attend on him thither, which Sir Anthony did consent unto.[11]

One might guess that this meeting was not accidental at all, but arranged by the Venetian authorities, and further guess that they might even have subsidised the new project, since Sherley by this time, with his extravagant lifestyle, might have been attracted by the offer of a Venetian contribution. We are told that there was another meeting with the Doge who 'urged it [i.e. Sir Anthony's visit to Persia] as a matter most necessary and of weighty consequences, promising to signify his allowance and opinion thereof to my Lord Marshal [Essex].'[12]

The question arises whether Sherley himself actually informed Essex about his new plan before he set off, and whether he explicitly received the Earl's backing. Certainly he said he did. In fact, in his autobiographical account of his travels he claimed that Essex had suggested the project: 'He proposed unto me (after a small relation which I made unto him from Venice) the voyage of Persia.'[13] This, however, contradicts a report made by Thomas Chaloner, one of Essex's agents in Italy, who met Sherley shortly before he left Venice, and was told about his plans. Chaloner clearly approved of Sherley and his project, and he tried to explain to Anthony Bacon, Essex's secretary, why Sherley was planning to make this journey on his own initiative. He wrote:

> I thought it convenient to advertise you, and withal to discharge part of so much as was committed to my charge by Sir Anthony Sherley at his departure for Constantinople. Whose love and zealous affection to my Lord Marshal and yourself is so well known that it were in vain for me to make any long protestation thereof. Therefore, in excuse of his journey toward the Levant without especial order, and perhaps disagreeing from some letters received at Venice, I can by my particular knowledge certainly inform you that he left no stone unmoved or means untried to find employment in the state of Venice.[14]

The truth may be that Sherley felt fairly confident that Essex would approve the venture given his recent interest in trade with the East, but was perhaps in too much of a hurry to wait until he actually received the Earl's permission.

This was a highly risky scheme, and it was to determine the course of Sherley's entire future life and well-being. To start with, their route lay across potentially hostile Turkish territory, the Persians and the Ottoman Turks being antagonistic neighbours who were frequently at war with each other. Then again, very few Englishmen had ever been to Persia, and none had met the present ruler. The newly recruited interpreter, Angelo, had explained to Anthony that Shah Abbas welcomed foreigners, but what reliance could be put on that? How would they get to meet this powerful monarch, whose thoughts and beliefs were a total mystery? And if they did meet him what would they say to him, and how would he react? Sherley was no expert in questions of international trade; in fact, he had probably never given such matters a thought before coming to Venice. To sum up, he was apparently choosing to gamble, not only with his own life, but also with the lives of the gentlemen and their servants who comprised his group and who were planning to go with him. At this point, too, another person invited to join Sir Anthony's party was his young brother, Robert, aged seventeen, who had been at the Grand Duke's court in Florence learning Italian.

So what might have been Sir Anthony's motives in choosing such an ambitious project? Certainly not any short-term financial gain. He may have believed that Essex, and also perhaps Queen Elizabeth, would support him if his journey turned out to benefit English trade, as he hoped. But it was a huge risk all the same, and the decision to go was his, and only his. Yet this was a project worthy of Sherley's high opinion of himself and his capabilities. Even if it failed it was a great adventure, undertaken perhaps in the name of 'that unseen thing called honour'.

Chapter 5

Sir Thomas Sherley the younger

In this chapter we turn back to Sir Thomas junior, the eldest of the three Sherley brothers, whom we last met receiving a knighthood for services in Ireland (Chapter 2). This was towards the end of 1589, and over the next few years it is remarkable how the events of his life seem to imitate those of his brother Anthony.

In 1591 Thomas, while attending the court, met and fell in love with an aristocratic young widow, Frances Brooke, Lady Stourton. He informed all his relatives that he intended to marry this lady, and it was generally accepted by them as a suitable match. However, he was then attracted to another, somewhat younger, lady. She was Frances Vavasour, one of the Queen's maids of honour, with whom he contracted a secret marriage while telling everyone that he was still bound to Lady Stourton. But news of his behaviour somehow became public, angering his father, as well as Sir Robert Cecil, who happened to be Lady Stourton's brother-in-law. 'I am almost overcome,' wrote old Sir Thomas to Cecil, 'in regard of the most unhappy wretched dealing of my unworthy boy.'[1] Queen Elizabeth was even more angry. She was always enraged by the affairs and marriages of her maids of honour, especially when they tried to keep them secret, and the result of her anger was that Thomas spent several weeks in the Marshalsea prison. However, he did eventually marry Frances Vavasour, and, so far as we know, the marriage was a happy one, in spite of the long periods when Thomas was abroad. This was in contrast with the earlier (secret) marriage of his brother Anthony to yet another Frances from the court. Frances Vavasour was to bear Thomas three sons and four daughters before her death in 1606 (for Anthony's opinion of Frances Vavasour, see Chapter 14).

One added complication of this episode was that Frances Vavasour, before her marriage to Thomas Sherley, had been the lover of Robert Dudley, the illegitimate son of the Earl of Leicester who had died two years earlier. Dudley was a tall, good-looking youth, and somewhat a favourite of the Queen. It seems that in spite of any potential rivalry over Frances, Thomas Sherley and Dudley became good friends at court. Later, having finally failed to inherit any of his father's property, due to his low birth, Dudley was to emigrate to Florence, where once again he was to play a small part in Thomas Sherley's life.

After a few years of domestic life, Thomas became aware that the Sherley family, in spite of the income from their estates, was approaching financial ruin. By 1597 his father was in deep trouble because a Privy Council examination of the records he had kept as Treasurer at War showed that he owed the Queen a large sum of money which he could not pay. Was there any way that young Thomas could retrieve the family fortunes? What occurred to him, just as it had to his brother the year before, was to take to the sea and lead a privateering expedition. He would need to borrow capital, probably from merchants prepared to gamble on his future success, and then purchase or hire ships, and recruit sailors and soldiers to man them. To do all this he needed the legal authorisation to mount such an expedition. Anthony had achieved this by obtaining a commission that stated he was part of an official government project to attack the Spanish fleet in Cádiz, but this was now impossible. The only way for Thomas was to apply for a letter of marque.

These documents, also known as letters of reprisal, had been available under English law for centuries, but had become highly popular in the second half of Elizabeth's reign. Theoretically, they merely gave a merchant whose goods had been stolen on the high seas the right to demand goods of equivalent value from any ship belonging to the nation guilty of the original theft. However, during these days of open hostility to Spain they were used as certificates allowing an English captain to seize any goods being traded with Spain or Portugal, or to pillage Spanish or Portuguese settlements anywhere in the world (Portugal being under the Spanish monarch from 1580 onwards). If a question arose about whether the goods seized were in fact Spanish, or rather belonged to a neutral country, the case was to be decided in the Court of Admiralty. By this date there were dozens of ship captains who set off from English ports hoping to make their fortunes in this way, though it should be said that most of them were professional seamen, unlike the two Sherley brothers.

Thomas managed to persuade a London merchant named John Skinner to invest in his project, and he also borrowed money from friends, including £100 from Robert Cecil. He acquired a small squadron of vessels, and over the next couple of years, between 1598 and 1600, made a number of short expeditions into the North Sea and beyond, looking for foreign merchant ships which he could capture and bring back to an English port as prizes, and whose cargoes he could then sell off.

However, his lack of experience meant that things often went wrong. His sailors frequently disobeyed him and became mutinous, and there were even occasions when the entire crew of one of his ships decided to leave his command and go off on their own. Also, he was not very good at deciding which merchant ships he was entitled to capture. For instance, on his first voyage he took four ships belonging to the German port of Lübeck and brought them back to Southampton. However, their owners complained that Lübeck was neutral in the wars between Spain and England, and that their cargoes were merely salt and cork for the fishing industry, which on examination proved to be correct. But Thomas persisted, arguing he felt sure that under the salt and cork there was hidden money and other valuables destined for Spanish forces in the Netherlands. One of the ships had to be entirely dismantled to prove him wrong. All four ships from Lübeck were eventually returned to their owners, and Thomas had to bear the costs.[2] During his first six months as a privateer he brought back seven ships, but none of them actually turned out to be lawful prizes.

The fourth of Sir Thomas's voyages was the most ambitious so far. It started badly, because one of his ships, the *Lion*, was entering the port of Falmouth when the captain decided to fire a cannon to announce their arrival. The cannon burst, killing two men and tearing up the deck, and the *Lion* had to be repaired while the rest of the squadron waited. Instead of looking for prizes at sea, on this occasion Thomas decided to loot some settlements on the Portuguese mainland. The villages were easily captured, but nothing of any value was discovered. 'Sir Thomas Sherley is returned with his navy royal.' wrote John Chamberlain, a prolific letter writer, 'and yesterday with his Lieutenant General Colonel Sims, posted to the court, as though they had brought tidings of the taking of Seville or some such town, whereas God knows they have but sacked two poor hamlets of two dozen houses in Portugal, the pillage whereof he gave to his army, reserving to himself only two or three peasants to ransome, of whom when he saw he could raise nothing, he would not bring them away for shame.'[3]

In the autumn of 1602, after several months rest, Sir Thomas decided to try his luck again, and this time to plunder Turkish possessions in the Mediterranean. By now both he and his father were in touch with James VI of Scotland, as were many other Englishmen looking to the future, including his brother Anthony and also Sir Robert Cecil. In a letter to James written some time later, when James had become king of England, and Sir Thomas was hoping he might help obtain release from a Turkish prison, he explained that the entire purpose of this new voyage had been to obtain suitable funding for the king-to-be by pillaging Turkish territory, and that he and his father had discussed this matter with Scottish diplomats in London. 'We all did greatly wish,' he wrote, 'some good means to be found to furnish your Majesty with a round sum of money. Many debates there were to that purpose and no likely way could be thought of, till I offered to hazard my life and estate to attempt to take from the Turk his treasure and lay it down (being taken) at Your Majesty's feet.'[4]

It seems highly unlikely that helping the new monarch with his finances ever crossed Thomas's mind at the time, but in any case he set off in October 1602, on what was to be his last privateering voyage. Again, he had managed to assemble a squadron of three ships, with a small force of soldiers on board. Passing through the Straits of Gibraltar, they attacked and plundered a Venetian merchant vessel, and then made for the port of Leghorn (now Livorno) in Tuscany. The point of going there was that Thomas expected a welcome from Ferdinand, Grand Duke of Tuscany, who was already engaged in intermittent war against Turkish shipping. Also, Robert Dudley, his friend from court, had become close to the duke, and was now based in Leghorn, designing warships for the Florentine navy.

For the events of this voyage, we have to rely on the possibly overdramatised account of Anthony Nixon, who published a popular booklet about the Sherley brothers in 1607 (see Chapter 12). The following quotations are from Nixon's unpaginated text, and he may well have got his information from Thomas himself. According to Nixon, Duke Ferdinand did give Thomas a warm welcome, but when he set sail again he tried to capture a large merchant ship near Gibraltar, which resulted in an eight-hour battle and the loss of over a hundred of his men. He returned to Leghorn to recuperate, and there his crews met other merchants who 'corrupted his men and made them mutinous,' explaining what a bad leader Sir Thomas was, and that 'he failed of warrant and authority for his proceedings'. English merchants in Leghorn were concerned that Sherley intended to raid Turkish possessions, 'whereupon will follow the overthrow of all English intercourse in the dominion of Turkey.' When the little squadron set out again, this time for the 'Archipelago' (i.e. the Greek islands in the Aegean, most of which were under Turkish control) two of Thomas's ships deserted him and went off on their own, and even on his one remaining ship he was 'much perplext with the contemptuous & unruly behauiour of his men,' who 'plainly told him that they would be no longer under his command.'

To placate his mutinous crew Sir Thomas proposed they should plunder a village on the small Greek island of Zea (now Kea) to the east of Athens. He landed a hundred men near the village, whereupon all the villagers fled with what possessions they could carry. But while his men were searching the houses for valuables, the natives counter-attacked, and Sir Thomas ordered a retreat. Instead of an orderly withdrawal all rushed back towards the ship, abandoning their leader and two sailors who stayed with him. Nixon takes up the story:

> Sir Thomas, having ten Greeks assailing him at once (only accompanied with two that could not escape) forced himself to make way through them, bestowing his blows on all sides, that the Islanders themselves well perceived, how hard a matter it had been for them to have overthrown, or defeated his company, if the rest had retained his courage and resolution. But he being overcharged with multitudes, was in the endeavour wounded and beaten downe: where being thus taken, and disarmed, they only can judge, that have undergone the like danger, what thoughts possessed his mind, when in this change of Fortune he found himself "forsaken of his own men & now in the hands of a trustless, bloody, and barbarous people."

Of the ten Greeks who had captured Sir Thomas, nine, says Nixon, were in favour of killing him and his two companions straight away, but the tenth persuaded them not to. Instead, they were tied up and imprisoned in the village, and later taken in an open boat to the much larger island of Negroponte (now Euboea). Although his mutinous crew remained at anchor off Zea for three days, they made no attempt to rescue their leader or even negotiate with the Greeks for his release. From Negroponte Sir Thomas wrote for help to everyone he knew who might petition the Turkish authorities for his release. He tried Robert Cecil's elder brother, Thomas, who had succeeded his father as Lord Burghley, and whom he had actually never met, giving him a new explanation as to why he had landed in Zea:

> I am a man unknown unto your Lordship ... but a gentleman, a knight & household servant of the Queen, my father is a man of good living, but something cast behindhand by hard fortune. I am his oldest son, and since his disgrace I have travailed to get my livings by my sword, and the labour of my hands. In handling which course I have thrust into ye Straightes with two ships which are holly myne own. I have done nothing prejudicial to any of her Majesties friends, only sought to make my voyage upon ye Spaniards, in which pretences whilst I did labour, my ship sprang a great leak, so I was forced to put into Zea.[5]

At Negroponte the Turkish authorities sent word of Sir Thomas's capture to Constantinople, where the city's pasha, or governor, decided the prisoner might be worth a ransom, and sent four soldiers to collect him and bring him to the capital. We look again to Nixon for details of poor Thomas's journey:

> Betweene Nigro Ponte and Constantinople is five hundreth miles, & all that way he was carried vpon a Moyle [mule], riding upon a pack-saddle with a great galley chaine about his legs, and another about his waist, and many times his legs bound under the horse belly, sometimes he lay in houses, sometimes under trees, and whensoever he lay in any town where there were any stocks, there they lodged him: & when they failed of such a place, they bound his legs together with a little chain, besides the great chaine about his waist, & his hands fast locked with manacles of iron.

In Constantinople he was interviewed by the vizier. Nixon proceeds to a description of Sir Thomas's rough handling in the Turkish capital after he claimed that neither he nor his family could pay the enormous ransom of 50,000 chequins[6] demanded by the Turks. He was threatened with execution and returned to his prison, 'Whereupon, the next morning at breake of day he was remooved to a worser place, and both his feet put into the Stockes, a great iron chaine about his neck, both his hands tied before him, and his body stretcht out all along, with a great sharpe stone laied under the reins of his back; so that it was impossible for him to stir, being also vexed continually with lice, which was not the least torment he endured: so that he often wished that the sentence of his death had been pronounced.'

After three days of this torture he was summoned back to the vizier who again asked for a 50,000 chequins ransom, and when Sir Thomas gave him the same answer he was sent back to prison and told he would certainly be beheaded. Soon afterwards, while preparing himself for death, he received a surprise visit from a Jewish merchant who said he had heard about his case and wanted to give him some advice. The merchant suggested he should agree to pay the ransom, and then find excuses to delay paying. After all, said the merchant, circumstances might change; either his royal patron, James, might agree to pay, or the vizier himself, who was known to have recently offended Sultan Mehmet II, might be dismissed. So Sherley followed this advice, promising to pay 40,000 chequins over a period of time if his treatment was improved and he was given better quarters and a servant. This was agreed, and the English ambassador, Henry Lello, who had already petitioned the Sultan on his behalf, continued to work for his release. The Jewish merchant's advice was sound because it turned out that it was the vizier, rather than Sir Thomas, who was beheaded, and this was shortly followed by the death of Sultan Mehmet, who was succeeded by his young son, Ahmet.

To cut a long story short, in December 1605, Sir Thomas received his release, due to a direct appeal to Sultan Ahmet by James I. 'Not withstanding this man's fault,' declared the new sultan to Lello, 'I present him to the King of England.' Because he was very ill, Thomas passed several weeks at Lello's house, and did not leave Constantinople until the following February. Then he spent considerable time visiting his friends in Venice and Florence, and did not arrive in England until the end of 1606.

As one might expect, Sir Thomas did not have a very high opinion of the Turks. After his release he made it his main purpose in life to attack the

Ottoman Empire, and in particular English trade with Turkey. He wrote a treatise on the evils of this trade, which now seems to be lost, although a book he also wrote, which was only published three centuries later, entitled *Discourse on the Turks*, may contain a watered-down version of it.[7] Here, he accused English merchants who traded with the Turks of selling them Christian slaves, and of directly harming the interests of their own country by providing them with guns and ammunition, a commercial transaction that he describes as 'abominable & naughte, & bringeth mutche sclaunder to our nation & religion ... There are no Christian ships that trade with the Turke that wyll carre any of these, but onely the Englishe.'[8] Sir Thomas also wrote letters to various contacts abroad explaining what he was doing to try and stop this pernicious trade. 'I make no doubt but to shake the foundation of the trade of the English in those parts,' he wrote to a Venetian friend.[9]

These letters ended up in the hands of Robert Cecil (now Lord Salisbury), who saw them as a direct attack on English interests. So, nine months after being freed from a Turkish prison, Sir Thomas found himself under interrogation in the Tower of London, where he defended his conduct with vigour. On his release he faced a more intractable, long-term problem. The Wiston estate, where his old father still lived, was heavily encumbered with debt, and when old Sir Thomas died some years later, young Sir Thomas, as the eldest son, inherited the estate, but also the debts. It became impossible for the Sherleys to retain their ancestral properties, and eventually young Thomas sold up and moved to the Isle of Wight where he obtained a position as Keeper of the Royal Park, and where there lived a wealthy relative, Sir John Oglander.

By now Sir Thomas had married a widow, Judith Taylor; his first wife, Frances, having died earlier. His expenses must have been considerable as we know he brought up eighteen children in total, seven by Frances and eleven by Judith. From time to time Oglander lent money to his poverty-stricken cousin, who died in 1633, the same year as his brother Anthony, to whose story we now return. 'To the Jacobean public he [Thomas] was something of a hero; he had defied the terrible Turk,' wrote Samuel Chew. 'But to our taste he is not an attractive figure; a dangerous, headstrong, and yet ineffectual buccaneer in his adventurous days; a nonetity [sic] thereafter.'[10]

Chapter 6

The journey to Qazvīn

On 24 May 1598, Sir Anthony's party, including his brother Robert, embarked from Malamocco, a small port near Venice. There were about twenty-six of them, most of whom were servants. Their journey to Persia was full of difficulties and dangers, and was to last more than six months. Sherley himself wrote an account of this journey and so did other members of the party – the two Englishmen, William Parry and George Manwaring, and also a mysterious Frenchman, Abel Pinçon, who may have been one of Robert Cecil's agents.[1] Pinçon joined the group in Venice and seems to have left it when they were in Russia, on their return journey from Persia.[2] One might therefore imagine their adventures were fairly well covered, but problems still arise about whose version of events to accept at particular moments. Anthony's version seems to have been written several years later than the others, and it is possible that when his account was to be published he embellished the narrative to make it more exciting. He introduces a series of enemies who threaten the group's progress, and also benefactors who suddenly arrive to help them out. For example, we hear from Anthony that there was a certain evil Portuguese merchant called Hugo de Potso who caused them all kinds of trouble early on in their journey, but who luckily died just when he was approaching Aleppo to confront them again. None of the other accounts mention this villain.

Anthony's account may be exciting, but it does not give us the lively descriptions of what they saw or learnt on their journey through Turkey, which the others do. Towards the beginning of his travel narrative, Anthony explains that as a superior gentleman he is not going to give us a mere anecdotal accounts of things he saw on the journey, 'which I did not behold with the eyes of a common Pilgrim or Merchant which make their judgement upon the superficial appearance of what they see, but as a Gentleman bred up in such experience, which hath made me somewhat capable to penetrate into the perfection and imperfection of the State, and into the good and ill Orders by which it is governed.'[3]

For the first leg of their expedition the party joined a ship that was sailing to Turkey via the island of Zante (today Zakinthos) in company with others, including a large contingent of Italian merchants. The journey to Zante was supposed to take ten days, but because of adverse winds it lasted more than twice as long, which meant that Sherley's group ran out of provisions long before they arrived. The Italians refused to help them out, but luckily some Persians kindly gave them enough food to last them until Zante.

Before the food crisis there arose another incident which started when it was reported that an Italian had 'used some villanous and oppobrious speaches towards our Queenes Majestie'. When Sir Anthony heard about this he had the culprit soundly flogged, so soundly in fact that, according to one witness, 'it is impossible he should ever recover'. Whereupon the other Italians all appeared in his support, fully armed, 'being in number some three score persons and we but four and twenty. Howbeit we were (with weapons drawn) pressed to defend and offend.' The captain of the ship then asked Sir Anthony how he dared behave like this on the ship which he, the captain, commanded, to which Anthony replied that it was 'an injury tending to the reproach and indignity of his Sovereign which he neither would nor could endure.' Then young Robert Sherley 'gave the captain a sound box,' but some other merchants eventually managed to pacify all parties.[4] However, this was not the end of the affair. When they reached Zante Sherley's group all got off the ship to buy food. The captain then sent their luggage after them, trained his guns on their boat, and told them that if they tried to return to the ship he would sink them. He did this 'through the instigation of one Hugo de Potso, a Portingall Factor [i.e. Portuguese merchant].'[5]

While they were shipless in Zante Anthony wrote to Henry Lello, the same English ambassador at Constantinople who was to help his brother Thomas. According to what Lello later reported to Robert Cecil, Sherley explained 'how he was sent by her Highness towards the Red Sea to meet with a fleet of Hollanders that are gone thither under color of traffick [i.e. pretending to be merchants],' and requiring me, added Lello, 'to send him, the Grand Signor [the Turkish Sultan] his commandment or pass through his dominions, which accordingly I have done.'[6] This was the same explanation for his journey that Sherley had produced when he was in Venice, except that he was now definitely claiming he was acting under orders from the Queen. It was also what he later told the English

The journey to Qazvīn

merchants in Aleppo (see below). No wonder that when Cecil heard Sherley was claiming royal authority for his project, this made him even less popular in in the eyes of himself and the Queen.

They managed to hire another ship ('an open Greek fishing boat, so old that the timbers were rotting'[7]) which took them first to Crete, which belonged to Greece, and where the ship they had bought needed a repair. There the group seems to have enjoyed themselves: 'we were kindly used amongst the citizens, but especially by the gentilwomen, who oftentimes did make us banquets in their gardens, with music and dancing.'[8] Unfortunately, they now had to sail eastwards to Cyprus, which was under Turkish control. Sherley clearly hated the Turks – or at least he did later, when he wrote his memoirs. He says he felt sorry for the native Greeks whom the Turks treated like slaves. He spent some time in his narrative explaining how easy it would be for the 'Princes Christian' to invade Cyprus and evict the Turks. We continue with Anthony's highly dramatic version of events.

The group travelled first to Paphos and then to Salamis at the north-east end of the island. There they had the bad luck to meet up again with the ship that had first taken them from Venice to Zante. On it was, of course, their enemy, Potso, who went to see the Turkish governor and told him that they were pirates, and very rich. He suggested the governor arrest them and confiscate their loot. But this conversation was overheard by some Armenians who knew them already, and they were so shocked that a Christian could betray other Christians to a Moslem that 'with all speed possible they [the Armenians] hired a Boate themselves, came with it unto us, provided in it victuals for us, and beseeched us, with tears in their eies, to flye from thence with all speed' (those who decide to help Sir Anthony often have tears in their eyes). Sherley and his friends took this advice, but they were chased by a boat full of Turkish soldiers dispatched by the governor, and it was only the coming of night that allowed their escape. It happened to be a clear, moonlit night, but even so 'our master' [who had hired the boat to them, and was steering it] managed to miss the entrance to the port of Alexandretta (Scanderoon) on the Turkish mainland, where they were supposed to be heading, and instead went on to Tripoli some miles to the south. There they were told that another boat which they had been following had been seized by pirates 'who put all to the sword,' and they realised that 'this certainly, was a great worke of God to preserve us'.[9] Throughout his story, Sherley is always conscious that God was watching out for them.

Returning to Alexandretta, they sailed up the Orontes river to Antioch, and from there on to Aleppo, a journey of six days during which they were accompanied and protected from thieves by some Turkish janissaries, friends of their interpreter, Angelo Corrai. Aleppo was an important trading depot on the silk road from China to Europe. Here, foreign merchants bought and sold goods of every description, from Persian silk to spices from India and further east. Traders from many nations lived and operated in the city, including fourteen English merchants from the Levant Company, headed by Richard Coulthurst, the English consul. Sherley and his party were given generous hospitality by them during the five weeks they stayed in Aleppo while they waited for a suitable caravan to set out for Baghdad, which they could join. These English merchants were particularly welcoming because they believed Sherley's story that he had been sent by Queen Elizabeth, and that his purpose was to reduce the Portuguese domination of trade with the East. At this time, too, the overland trade through Aleppo was under threat from a new sea route, pioneered by Portuguese explorers, round the Cape of Good Hope.

Aleppo, with its busy streets and vast souks (markets), was a multi-ethnic city in which, inevitably, there was the possibility of racial conflict. When Othello is about to kill himself he refers to an earlier encounter with a Turk, which an Elizabethan audience probably saw as typical:

> And say besides that in Aleppo once,
> Where a malignant and a turbaned Turk
> Beat a Venetian and traduced the state,
> I took by the throat the circumsized dog
> And smote him – thus! (he stabs himself)[10]

Sherley's companions also experienced street violence. George Manwaring, who was staying in Coulthard's house, describes an incident which he claims was typical: 'I met with a Turk, a gallant man he seemed to be by his habit, and saluting me in this manner – took me fast by one of the ears with his hand, and so did lead me up and down the streets; and if I did chance to look sour upon him, he would give me such a wring, that I did think verily he would have pulled off my ear, and this he continued with me for the space of one hour, with much company following me, some throwing stones at me, and some spitting on me.' But Manwaring had his revenge: 'returning to the Consul's house, the Consul's Janizary, seeing me all bloody, asked me how I came hurt; I told him the manner of it. He presently in a rage did take his staff in his hand and bade me go with him.' They found the Turk 'sitting with some gentlemen,' and the janissary 'ran fiercely to him, and threw him on his back, giving him twenty blows on his legs and his feet, so that he was not able to go or stand.' Manwaring adds 'in this sort our men were served divers times.'[11]

Sherley got on well with the Levant Company merchants. So well, in fact, that he was able to borrow from them a large sum of money. This is reported by one of them, William Clark, although he himself was not particularly enthusiastic about the loan: 'he [Sir Anthony] hath here taken up of the whole company 3,000 dollars to be repaid the treasurer [of the Levant Company] in England by the Earl of Essex, whereof we have no doubt but good payment will be made, yet for my own part was not over willing to give my consent."[12] Part of this sum was spent by Sir Anthony on acquiring English cloth and jewellery so as to help them all disguise themselves as merchants on the next stage of their journey. Declaring he was a merchant, he then applied to the pasha of the city for a pass allowing them to proceed towards Baghdad, which was granted.

Shortly before they left Aleppo, Anthony received some disquieting news. Apparently his old enemy, de Potso, had discovered where they were and was on his way to Aleppo to make more trouble. But yet again God intervened on the side of the English merchants: 'And though that Hugo de Potso threatened as much as an ill mind, and great purse could make him hope to prevail against me ... yet ever the first providence, which saved me before, determined so well also for me then, that four miles from Aleppo he died.'[13] That may have been the end of Potso, but one or two of the local Turkish despots they were to meet on the journey were to prove even worse.

In early September 1598 they left Aleppo, having hired horses for themselves, and mules and donkeys for their baggage. They were to be part of a large caravan consisting of Turkish officials as well as merchants from various nations. During the long days and weeks ahead, no doubt Sherley got to know many of his new companions. One of them, a Florentine named Victorio Speciero, 'whom I had only known in the way between Aleppo and Babylon by a riding acquaintance,'[14] was later to save them from disaster. The caravan travelled overland to Bira on the Euphrates where they waited for boats to be prepared, and then spent twenty-three days gliding slowly down the river in a convoy of thirteen boats, stopping and pitching camp each night. The three 'journalists' continued to describe in their journals whatever they thought might interest their readers: the ruined towers of ancient Babylon; a bubbling lake of blackest bitumen; the game of polo, 'their horses are so well trained to this that they run after the ball like cats'. Anthony, on the other hand, considered himself above such trivial descriptions, as he tells us again in his account of the journey: 'To tell wonders, of things I saw, strange to us, that are borne in these parts, is for a Traveller of another profession than I am, who had my end to see, and make use of the best things, not to feed myself, and the world, with such trifles.'[15]

Near the town of Rakka (Raqqa) an incident occurred which might easily have ended in disaster for all of them. Manwaring explains that when approaching the town

> it was our order in all our boats to give a volley of shot, and doing the like at that place, one of the Turks had charged his piece with a bullet, which bullet did kill one of the King's guard, being walking along the side of the river with some fifty more of his fellows, who did draw their swords in a rage, not knowing who to take revenge upon; but the Turk that killed him, standing up, cried with a loud voice, saying it was one of the Christians that killed him; whereupon they came all towards our boat, swearing they would kill us every man.

Luckily, 'a Turk of Mahomet's kindred [perhaps the muezzin from a mosque] shouted to the guard, "there is your fellow, for I saw him put the bullet into his piece"; which caused them to make a stand; but, on the sudden they all ran fiercely upon him, and cut him into a hundred pieces, taking the pieces and throwing them up and down.'[16]

A couple of days after this narrow escape they came up against a local ruler who, when Sherley told him they were English merchants, insisted on viewing their merchandise, 'which we (God wot) durst not contradict: and so he borrowed (without a privy seal or bill of his hand) some thirty yards of the cloth of silver until our return.' However, no other problems ensued, except for two members of the group, Robert Browne and William Kydman, who managed to get on the wrong side of Sir Anthony. This was a rather mysterious affair which is not dealt with in any of the other accounts of the journey, and comes to light only in a couple of letters in the Cecil Papers, and a reference in the *Letter Book of William Clark*, the Aleppo merchant mentioned earlier in this chapter. 'Sir Anthony Sherley being within eight days journey of Babylon [often used as an alternative name for Baghdad] upon the river Euphrates,' wrote Clark, 'it so happened that some discontent came betwixt some of his company, whereupon he put two of them ashore who passed the desert in great misery and danger, being robbed and stripped naked by the Arabs, and forced to go so two days journey without any food. So five days past they came into Aleppo in miserable case, God knoweth. They remain at our consul's until the coming of the [ship] *Angel*.'[17]

Sir Anthony had written to Richard Coulthurst, the Aleppo consul, asking him to imprison Browne and Kidman until they could be sent back to England, which was done. In his letter he gives a somewhat vague account of what the two were guilty of: 'I must charge you with the safe, close & discreet keeping of these two fellows, not only for the horrible intention to deny Christ, but also for great treasons contrived against her Majesty's person, the articles of which, subscribed by six of the best witnesses here, I will send you by my brother.'[18]

Sherley never did send his brother back to Aleppo with the evidence, and we have no way of hearing Browne and Kydman's side of the story (except for a subsequent letter from Kydman to Robert Cecil protesting his innocence and 'how maliciously we are dealt with by Sir Anthony Sherley'). The whole episode leaves an unpleasant taste in the mouth, and seems to be another example (like flogging the Italian on the voyage to Zante) supporting the judgement that Sir Anthony was 'an irascible man, opinionated, truculent and turbulent'.[19] There will be other examples.

At Falluja they left the river and proceeded overland towards Baghdad. There they were closely interrogated by the pasha of the city, and the goods they had brought with them inspected. The pasha then commandeered most of the cloth and jewellery for himself, offering them a price of less than half its value. Luckily, Sherley had already been warned by a Turkish official who had been travelling with them that such behaviour was likely, and the two of them had done a deal by which the official told the Baghdad authorities that part of Sherley's merchandise belonged to him. However, it also now became clear that the pasha suspected the English of not being merchants at all, so, to allay his doubts, Sherley told him that another consignment of his goods would arrive in Baghdad shortly. This led to the pasha – no doubt anticipating more half-price valuables – forbidding him to leave, and the group spent a month of enforced idleness in the city. To make things worse, they heard that the authorities in Aleppo had also come to believe they were not what they said they were, and had sent letters to Baghdad demanding their arrest.

For Sir Anthony this was the low point of the entire journey. He had spent all his money, was unable to continue his journey, and could expect nothing except imprisonment or worse, for himself and those who looked to him for leadership. In his journal he sums up his dire predicament:

> What extreme affliction I was in for the present, and what just cause of fear for the future, every man may easily judge. I had my brother with me, a young Gentleman whose affection to me had only led him to that disaster. I had also five and twenty others, Gentlemen for the most part ... I had no means to give them sustenance to live, and less hope to unwrap them from the horrible snare into which I had brought them, being far from all friends, not understanding the language of the people into whose hands I was fallen, much less their proceedings: only this much I knew, they were Turks, inhumane in their natures, and addicted to get by all means, just and unjust.[20]

At this critical moment Anthony produces a new saviour. This one was his 'riding acquaintance' from Baghdad, Victorio Speciero, who now warned him 'that there was a great muttering among divers great men [in Baghdad] as to what I was, and what my designs might be; that he found me to be dangerously spied after, and wished me to have regard if not to myself yet to so many [in my group].' At first Sherley was suspicious of this Italian, 'that I did rather imagine him to be the spy,' so he answered him politely but cautiously. However, Speciero spoke to him again later, telling him that a caravan of Persian pilgrims from Mecca had just arrived in the city, and that he and his companions would be wise to join them on their road to Persia. He said that he had no idea what Sherley's ambitions were, but was sure they 'were for some great end, which he did believe well of ... and taking me by the hand, beseeched me to believe him, and to go presently with him to the caravan, which I did.' There the Italian showed Anthony a contract for horses, camels and mules which he had hired for the group, and gave him 'a bag of Chakins [Turkish coins]'. His final service to them was to inform Turkish officials that Sherley was sick and would have to keep to his bed for several days. In the meantime they were able to join the caravan and leave the city unnoticed when it set out.[21] The rest of their journey was relatively straightforward, and soon they left Turkish territory. On the way through Persia they were well treated, especially when they explained that their mission was to meet the Shah in Qazvīn.

Chapter 7

Persia before Abbas

Shah Abbas, the king whom Anthony had come to meet, was born in 1571. This chapter looks briefly at the history of Persia before that date. The country has usually been called Iran by its citizens but – until recently – Persia by the rest of the world. I shall stick to Persia, and try to summarise its early history in a few paragraphs (which is virtually impossible, I know).

This history goes back far longer than that of most nations. When Cyrus the Great, king of Persia (559-530 BC) ruled an empire, probably the greatest the world had yet seen, that stretched from the Aegean sea in the west to the Indus river in the east, Britain was a patchwork of Iron Age tribes, with five centuries to go before the arrival of the Romans. Two of Cyrus' successors, Darius I and Xerxes, were also powerful and successful monarchs, even though they failed to conquer Greece in their two vast expeditions of 490 and 480 BCE.

> A King sate on the rocky brow
> Which looks o'er sea-born Salamis;
> And ships, by thousands, lay below,
> and men in nations:—all were his!
> He counted them at break of day—
> And when the sun set, where were they?
>
> *Byron*

Since that time Persia has endured a long history of invasions, wars, foreign rulers, and provinces lost and won. Easily the most significant of the foreign invaders were the Arabs in the seventh century AD, whose arrival led the Persians to convert to Islam. Since then, the country's boundaries continued to shift, and during much of the thirteenth century, through to the fifteenth, Persia ceased to exist as an independent unit, becoming merely part of the Mongol and then Timurid empires (i.e. the empire of Tamburlaine, or Timur-the-lame). Nevertheless, during all these centuries Persian culture and traditions survived, which is why Michael Axworthy, in his recent history of the nation, has suggested that Persia/Iran should be seen as an 'empire of the mind' rather than a physical state with settled boundaries.[1]

By the beginning of the sixteenth century Persia consisted of many different peoples speaking different languages. The Persian heartland extended from the southern shore of the Caspian Sea to the Persian Gulf. To the west, in lands now forming Azerbaijan, Armenia, and parts of Syria and Anatolia, lived Turkoman, Kurdish and other tribes, most speaking dialects relating to Turkish. It was horsemen from these warlike tribes who provided the backbone of Persian military power.

At this time there were many Sufi movements. Sufism, or Islamic mysticism, incorporated ideas outside the official religious mainstream, many of them partly derived from pre-Islamic sources such as Zoroastrianism, and condemned as heretical by the priests. Members of a Sufi group believed that under the guidance of their 'perfect leader' any disciple might follow the spiritual path and ultimately share a mystical union with the divine. Another fundamental tenet was about the nature of time. While monotheistic religions – Islam, Judaism, Christianity – held that time was a continuous narrative leading to end-time and divine judgement, Sufis thought time was cyclical, like the succession of the seasons or the movement of the stars and planets. Some held that an Arab cycle of time which had started with the birth of Mohammad was about to end, giving way to a Persian cycle, which would lead to new insights about God and the universe. Many Sufis also believed in reincarnation – that adepts might retain memories of their past lives, and thus make spiritual progress through the centuries. Sufism attracted Turkoman tribesmen by providing an emotional and personal spiritual experience in contrast to the orthodox, and more impersonal, versions of Islam offered by the *ulema*, or priestly hierarchy.[2]

The Safavid dynasty, which was to rule Persia throughout the coming century, originated as one of these local Sufi orders. It was based at Ardabil, close to the modern Azerbaijan/Persian border, and was led by hereditary Sufi leaders claiming descent from Mohammad, and regarded by their devoted followers as participating in the divinity of God. The movement had been started by Sheikh Safi ud-Din, who lived two centuries earlier, giving his name to the Safavids.

What distinguished the Safavid movement from other Sufi groups was its success in recruiting large numbers of disciples from outside the Ardabil region, and then gradually changing from an essentially spiritual society into one which also had political and military ambitions. The combination of the warlike skills shown by these semi-nomadic Turkoman tribesmen, coupled with their devotion and obedience to their leader, made them into an invincible force which was able to conquer increasingly large swathes of territory south-east of the Caspian sea. Safavid horse-warriors were called *Qizilbash,* meaning 'red heads' after the distinctive red caps with twelve folds which they wore. The caps symbolised devotion to their Sufi leader as well as to the twelve Imams worshipped by the Shi'ite branch of Islam (see below). Most of the land captured by the Safavids was portioned out to tribal leaders (amirs) under a form of feudalism whereby they collected and owned the revenue received from taxation. Much like feudal nobility in the West, their obligation to their Sufi head was to produce an agreed number of mounted warriors to serve him when called on to do so.[3]

In 1501 Ismail I succeeded his father as head of the Safavids. He was the ancestor of Shah Abbas the Great, and his policies were crucial in establishing the kind of nation that Abbas would one day inherit. Like his son Tahmasp after him, and like Abbas many years later, Ismail had to survive a dangerous childhood. His father and elder brother were both killed when fighting a powerful confederation of tribes called the *Aq Qoyonlu* (White Sheep). Ismail at the age of seven had to be taken into hiding, from which he emerged ten years later to assume leadership of the Safavid movement. From early on he proved a capable and charismatic leader of his Qizilbash followers.

For the next two decades Ismail was involved in war. His horsemen launched successful attacks against rival Sufi groups and also against the White Sheep, and the lands under his control were rapidly extended. As his territorial ambitions increased he succeeded in regaining much of what had once belonged to Persia but had been seized by independent groups and hostile neighbours – the Ottoman Turks to the west, and Uzbek tribes to the east. By 1510 he had restored the former boundaries of the nation, and in the same year his army ambushed and destroyed a larger force of Uzbeks who were advancing from Khorasan, killing their commander (whose skull Ismail is said to have made into a drinking cup). Soon afterwards he was in a position to declare himself Shah of

Persia before Abbas

Persia, with his capital at Tabriz. He had morphed his Sufi movement into an established nation-state, all the while retaining the passionate loyalty and enthusiasm of the Qizilbash, who continued to believe in the divine mission of their leader.

It mattered little to his followers that ruthlessness and cruelty were outstanding characteristics of this dynamic young Shah. His treatment of those who surrendered to him was similar to that of the Mongol hordes who had occupied Persia three centuries earlier. I quote from a recent history of Persia:

> In at least two mountain fortresses in Mazandaran province which fell to the Qizilbash army in 1504, Ismail reportedly ordered the massacre of the entire population, perhaps in vengeance for their stiff resistance. In the same campaign, after the capture of the fortress of Usta in the central Alborz range, where Morad Beg Bayandori, the last of the Aq Qoyonlu princes, and a blood relative of Ismail, had taken refuge, the Safavid conqueror ordered his wild Qizilbash devotees to broil the prince alive and devour him. Upon defeating the local Persian dynasty of Shervan in the lower Caucasus [part of the White Sheep federation], against whom both Ismail's father and grandfather had fought and died, he massacred the ruling family and exhumed and burnt the bodies of their ancestors, a practice he believed would deprive them of final redemption.[4]

Ismail's years of successful warfare ended suddenly when, in 1514, he faced a large Ottoman army at Chaldiran, north of Tabriz. His crushing defeat was largely due to the Turks' use of gunpowder. The Persian cavalry were devastated by heavy cannon, a weapon that the proud Quizilbash horsemen had until then looked down on and neglected. Ismail himself was wounded and his entire harem, including his favourite mistress, captured by the enemy. He retired to his palace, heart-broken, and from then on started looking for solace in bouts of heavy drinking. He also turned to religion, left the business of government to others, and never again participated in a military campaign. The Ottomans went on to capture Tabriz, although Safavid forces soon took it back from them. But the most important result of the defeat was that Ismail's aura of invincibility was punctured, and the Qizilbash tribes soon became hard to discipline, given to fighting among themselves. It would be left to his successors, Tahmasp, and especially Abbas, to drastically reduce the power of these unruly tribesmen.

Until now I have not mentioned Ismail's most important contribution to the future of his dynasty and of Persia, which was that he made Shi'ism the official religion of the country. Then, as today, the two main branches of Islam were the Shi'a and the Sunni. This division had started back in the seventh century, in the days of Mohammad himself. The term Shi'a is short for Shi'a Ali, the party of Ali, who was Mohammad's cousin and married his daughter, Fatima. The Shi'a were those who thought that Islam should be ruled by the blood descendants of Ali and Mohammad. They believed that Ali's succession had been usurped by corrupt forces who had installed a series of leaders called caliphs to command the ever-expanding Islamic world. Instead of these caliphs, the Shi'a – or the majority of them – held to a succession of twelve Imams who, it was claimed, were all personally descended from Mohammad. The twelfth Imam had to go into hiding (or 'occultation') when his father was murdered, but it was believed that one day he would return to the world. It was this 'Twelver Shi'ism' to which Ismail gave his support

The Shi'a have always seen themselves as the underdogs of history, betrayed and humiliated by the powerful Sunni majority. The most crucial moment in the Shi'a narrative was in 640 AD when a group led by Ali's son, Hussein, was travelling from Mecca to Baghdad when they were confronted by a large force of soldiers dispatched by the Sunni Caliph of Baghdad, Yazid. The soldiers demanded that the group swear allegiance to Yazid, and when Hussein refused they were attacked and all of them killed. The martyrdom of Hussein took place at Karbala in present-day Iraq, which, for Shi'ites, rivals Mecca as one of the holiest shrines in the Islamic world.

Before Ismail there were both Sunnis and Shi'ites in Persia, and even among the Qizilbash tribes, but Ismail made the important decision to enforce Twelver Shi'ism on the entire nation. As a result he received the support of the *ulema*, the group of senior Shi'a clergy. This alliance between the Shah and the *ulema* continued throughout the following centuries, right up to the fall of Mohammed Reza Shah in 1979. Ismail's decision also meant that to his Sufi charisma (somewhat tarnished after Chaldiran) was added his status as head of the official religion of

Persia. Another advantage was that Persians had now even more clearly distinguished themselves from their enemies across the borders, since both the Ottoman Turks to the west and the Uzbeks to the east were orthodox Sunnis, as were – and still are – the vast majority of Moslems throughout the world.

Ismail's policy had the effect of providing all Persians with a clear ideology to support and fight for. He lost no opportunity in attacking the faith of his enemies. For instance, he ordered the ritual cursing of the first three caliphs who, according to Shi'ites, had usurped the office that belonged to Ali and his Imam successors. 'Ismail had officials go through the streets carrying axes over their shoulders and crying out: "Cursed be Abu Bakr! Cursed be Omar! Cursed be Uthman!" Anyone who heard this was obliged, on pain of death, to express their approval.'[5]

Ismail died in 1524 leaving a son, Tahmasp, who was only ten when he succeeded to the throne. As with other Safavid rulers, there was a period of turmoil and infighting between the Quizilbash tribes while the Shah was still a boy, during which powerful amirs competed for power. However, when he came of age Tahmasp was able to enforce his will, and his reign lasted until his death in 1572 – longer than any other Safavid ruler. He was just as ruthless as his father had been in dealing with enemies, internal and external, but he continued Ismail's policy of supporting Twelver Shi'ism and the priestly establishment, rather than emphasising his divine powers as Sufi leader.

The early part of Tahmasp's reign coincided with that of the aggressive Ottoman Sultan known to history as Suleiman the Magnificent, who launched three massive invasions into western Persia. The Turks were only halted by Tahmasp's scorched earth policy of destroying farms and wells in the path of Suleiman's huge armies, so that each time they won victories against the Persians the Turks were forced to retreat owing to lack of supplies. Finally, in 1555 the treaty of Amasya was signed which ensured peace for the next fifty years, but which gave the Turks Mesopotamia – that is, much of present-day Iraq, including Baghdad. One result of these wars was that Tahmasp decided to move his capital from Tabriz, which was too vulnerable to future Turkish incursions, to Qazvīn, 300 miles to the east.

Another advantage of making Qazvīn the new capital was that it was situated in the Persian heartland, far away from the territory of the unruly Qizilbash. This move became part of Tahmasp's long-term policy of reducing the influence of these Turcoman tribes and their amirs. He also undertook a series of systematic invasions into the Caucasus region, bringing back thousands of young men and girls, mainly from Christian Georgia, whom he resettled in central Persia. They were known as *ghulams*, or slaves, and most of them were forced to convert to Islam. The advantage of these new soldiers for the Shah was that, unlike the Qizilbash, they owed obedience only to him, and had no tribal loyalties. Many of the men were conscripted into a new military force which, in the future, was to rival the Qizilbash. Other *ghulams* joined the growing bureaucracy of the Persian state, rising sometimes to high position, some even becoming provincial governors or personal advisers of the Shah. The supreme example was Allaverdi Khan, who was to become Shah Abbas's leading general. Of the girls, many entered harems owned by Persian nobles, and even the royal harem, where their political influence grew. Abbas would continue and develop this *ghulam* policy, thus creating a new layer of power in the Persian state.

In 1562 Anthony Jenkinson, a young merchant from the English Muscovy company, visited Tahmasp to try and persuade him to allow trade between England and Persia. Jenkinson had taken months to reach Qazvīn, having travelled via Moscow and Bukhara, and he had with him samples of English cloth as well as letters from Queen Elizabeth supporting his mission. But when he finally achieved his interview with the Shah it turned out that Tahmasp was not in a good mood, as is clear from Jenkinson's journal. Firstly, 'he demanded me in what language the letters were written, I answered in the Latin, Italian, and Hebrew: well said he, we have none within our realm that understand those tongues.' Later in the interview, Tahmasp turned to matters of faith: 'Then he reasoned with me much of religion, demanding whether I was a *gower*, that is to say an unbeliever, or a *Muselman*, that is, of Mahomet's law. Unto whom I answered that I was neither unbeliever nor Mahometan, but a Christian.' Tahmasp then wanted to know – or pretended he wanted to know, since most of the women in his harem came from Christian Georgia – what a Christian was, and when it had been explained to him, he pronounced his verdict: '"Oh thou unbeliever", said he, "we have no need to have friendship with the unbelievers", and so willed me to depart. I being glad thereof did reverence and went my way.'[6]

As will be discussed again in Chapter 10, there is an interesting contrast between the rejection of Jenkinson and the way that Anthony

Sherley would later be received by Tahmasp's grandson, Shah Abbas. Very likely, Tahmasp's treatment of Jenkinson had nothing to do with his faith, but was rather that he did not want to antagonise the Turks through whose territory all trade between Persia and the West then flowed, and with whom he had made the treaty of Amasya, as mentioned above. Jenkinson himself in his journal explained that if a trade deal between England and Persia 'came to the knowledge of the Turk, it should be a means to break their new league and friendship'.[7] Probably, the Shah was using differences in religion as an excuse to reject any discussions about trade. And in fact, a few years later when Tahmasp's relations with Turkey worsened, he did agree to a trade deal with the Muscovy company, but this did not last long, mainly because of the perils and difficulties of sending goods between England and Persia via Russia.

During his final years, Tahmasp, like his father Ismail before him, became obsessively religious. He gave up the work of government to others and retired to his palace at Qazvīn, refusing to meet his subjects. Without leadership the political situation deteriorated, and continued to do so during the brief reigns of the next two Shahs, Ismail II and Mohammad Khodabanda. It was not until Mohammad's son, Abbas, was able to take control that things started to improve. Nevertheless, the shahs discussed in this chapter, Ismail I and Tahmasp, left Abbas important legacies, two of which were the imposition of Shi'ism, and a start in reducing the power of the Qizilbash.

Chapter 8

The young Shah

The future Shah Abbas was born in Herat in January 1521, and spent the first sixteen years of his life in that city. Herat, now in Afghanistan, was then capital of the province of Khorasan, and one of Persia's richest and most beautiful cities. It was a commercial centre on the silk road from central Asia to the Mediterranean, and had been the capital of the fifteenth-century Timurid rulers, who had embellished the city with mosques and palaces.

> If any one ask thee which is the pleasantest of cities,
> Thou mayest answer him that it is Herat.
> For the world is like the sea, and the province of Khurāsān
> like a pearl-oyster therein,
> The city of Herāt being as the pearl in the middle
> of the oyster.
>
> *Rumi*[1]

Herat was also a forward defence for Mashad, the site of the holiest Shi'a shrine in Persia, as the burial place of the eighth Imam. But during the time of the Safavids Herat was under continuous threat from Uzbek tribes to the east. Therefore the shahs always installed a Safavid prince to be governor there, together with a powerful Qizilbash amir as his partner, or his guardian if he was too young to actually rule.

The father of Abbas was Mohammad Khodabanda, eldest son of Shah Tahmasp. He was said to be a pious, ascetic and gentle soul. When his younger self had suffered an eye disease that left him almost blind few thought he was ever likely to become the Shah. Abbas' mother was Mahd-e Olya, who was to prove herself a woman of energetic and stubborn character. Before Abbas was born, his father had been appointed governor of Herat, but when his son was only eighteen months old Khodabanda became involved in a dispute with his Qizilbash assistant, and to keep the peace Shah Tahmasp transferred him and his wife to Shiraz, hundreds of miles to the south. Abbas never saw his mother again, and his father only briefly, many years later. Instead of Khodabanda, Tamasp appointed his son, the baby prince, as titular governor of Herat.

We now turn to the confusing and violent events that darkened Abbas's childhood and adolescence. During this entire period the central government was weak and quarrelsome. Qizilbash tribes fought each other, using Safavid princes as figureheads in their struggle for power, while Persia's neighbours took advantage of the anarchy to launch attacks across the borders. This was especially true during Tahmasp's final years when he neglected the business of government and became virtually a religious recluse, isolated in his palace in Qazvīn. Also, he failed to name his successor, and consequently his sons became pawns in the hands of ambitious amirs. One faction, which included Tahmasp's forceful and ambitious daughter (and Abbas's aunt), Pari Khan Khanum, supported Tahmasp's second son, Prince Ismail, and another faction backed the third son, Prince Haidar. When Tamasp died, Haidar made an ill-planned attempt to seize power, which failed. Disguised as a woman, he attempted to hide from his enemies in the royal harem at Qazvīn, but the supporters of Ismail dragged him out of the harem and garrotted him. This unparalleled act of violence against the favourite son of their former Shah and spiritual leader sparked a complete breakdown of law and order in Qazvīn, where bands of Qizilbash fought each other in the streets, and barricades were set up in various parts of the city.

Now began the short and blood-stained reign of Shah Ismail II, who had spent eighteen years of his life in prison because his father, Tahmasp, suspected him of disloyalty. This experience had led to an acute paranoia whereby Ismail saw enemies everywhere, who had to be eliminated as possible rivals to the throne. He had several cousins as well as two of his younger brothers murdered, and another brother blinded. To the south, in Shiraz, the weak and pious father of Abbas, Mohammad Khodabanda, who was the oldest brother, was spared, probably because, being almost blind, he was not seen as a threat. Ismail's bloodthirsty ambitions now spread as far as Herat. He ordered the murder of several amirs belonging to one of the leading Qizilbash tribes, the Ustalju, because some of them had supported his brother, Haidar.

Abbas's first Qizilbash guardian was an Ustalju, although he had played no part in the previous factional struggle. But one day in the autumn of 1577, when Abbas was six years old, a group of horsemen from Qazvīn entered Herat, and, bursting into the house of the guardian, cut him to pieces before he could summon help. He was replaced by Ali Quli Khan, an amir from a rival tribe, the Shamlu. It was he and his wife who were to look after Abbas until he was sixteen, and who became the nearest the young boy ever had to a father and mother. Shortly after this, Shah Ismail II decided that Abbas, too, was a threat, and sent to Herat an order for his murder. But Ali Quli Khan took the enormous risk of disobeying the order, and, fortunately for him, Shah Ismail died before there could be repercussions. (He was found one morning dead in his bed, apparently from an overdose of opium, although there were suspicions that he had been poisoned by Pari Khan Khanum, his half-sister.) Thus it was by sheer accident that Abbas was spared from sharing the fate of his uncles and other relatives, at least nine of whom had been murdered or blinded by the Shah. All this, according to the Persian chroniclers, was part of God's plan for the future Shah Abbas.[2]

After Ismail II's death, violent power struggles between the tribes continued as before, the only difference being the involvement of the two powerful females, Abbas's mother and his aunt. In spite of his weak sight, Abbas's father, Mohammad Khodabanda, found himself placed on the throne as Shah Mohammad. Pari Khan Kanum, Abbas's aunt, assumed that she would now be the real power behind the throne, but had reckoned without Abbas's mother, Mahd-e Oliva, an equally determined woman, who immediately started to make all the important decisions. She wasted no time in disposing of her rival. Pari Khan Kanum was pulled out of the royal harem and strangled.

It was Mahd-e Oliva who then organised and dispatched an army to the Caucasus to stop the Ottomans overrunning Persian territory. Although this campaign was initially successful, the Qizilbash amirs resented her role, especially in military affairs, which they considered belonged to them. When she ordered them to follow up a victory by the pursuit of the enemy, many refused to obey. A group of amirs at the court in Qazvīn decided that she had to go. 'Your Majesty well knows,' they told Shah Mohammad, 'that women are notoriously lacking in intelligence, weak in judgement, and extremely obstinate.'[3] Eventually, soldiers again entered the harem to strangle both Mahd-e Oliva and her mother. Shah Mohammad, weak as ever, announced that he accepted his wife's murder as God's will. Abbas was about eight when his mother was murdered, and although he had not seen her since he was less than two years old, the news of her fate must have had a devastating effect on him, and perhaps made him start to understand that he and his future family would never be safe until the Qizilbash tribes had been brought under royal control.

During Shah Mohammad's reign his eldest son, Prince Hamza, who was Abbas's brother, increasingly ran the country. When another war broke out with the Ottoman Turks, leading to the fall of Tabriz, it was Hamza who led an army against the enemy. Tabriz, in north-eastern Persia, was the former capital of Persia, and its loss was a significant blow. Hamza displayed ability as a military commander, but some of the Qizilbash tribes, by now unaccustomed to a strong central government, were reluctant to obey his orders. In the middle of the campaign a group of disaffected amirs organised his assassination. One night, when Hamza lay in a deep sleep after an evening of drinking, his personal barber, whom he had trusted as a close friend, crept into his tent: 'After the close of a great supper party that had taken place in the royal pavilion, this murderous servant entered the prince's sleeping apartment without being perceived, very quietly, and forthwith cut his master's throat with all the skills of his barber's art.'[4]

Amirs at the court in Qazvīn now forced Shah Mohammad, much against his will, to pronounce his youngest son, Prince Abu Taleb, to be his heir, passing over Abbas in the line of succession. But events in Khorasan were to alter the picture. Abbas's guardian in Herat, Ali Quli Khan, quarrelled with Murshid Quli Khan, the governor of Mashad, who succeeded in seizing the seventeen-year-old Prince Abbas and carrying him off to Mashad. Meanwhile, Persia's old enemy in the east, the Uzbeks, launched another attack on Khorasan. Murshid now decided that the time had come to exploit his possession of Abbas, whom he proclaimed to be Shah instead of his father. Hearing that Shah Mohammad was away from the capital dealing with rebels to the south, Murshid set off towards Qazvīn with the young prince and a small force of horsemen. On the way he was joined by various amirs and their followers, who were opposed to those who had chosen Abu Taleb as Mohammad's heir. History was now repeating itself, with two factions of Qizilbash, each supporting their own Safavid prince.

When Abbas and Murshid approached Qazvīn they were greeted by large crowds expressing their support. Shah Mohammad and his army were 200 miles to the west, and the amirs who were with him when they heard the news of Abbas's arrival, could not agree what to do next. In his messages to them Murshid skilfully exploited these divisions, and soon the leaders of the Abu Taleb faction began to quarrel with each other. Many Qizilbash, realising the likely outcome, started to desert and make their way towards Qazvīn to pledge loyalty to their new leader. Eventually they were followed by Mohammad and Abu Talib, who, by the time they approached the city, had few followers left: 'When a group of leaders came out to meet them they found the Shah and Abu Taleb sitting in their tent, stunned by the mysterious workings of providence, and escorted them into the city. Prince Abbas greeted the Shah and Prince Abu Taleb at the royal palace; he kissed his father's hand, embraced his brother, and then escorted his father to the harem quarters.' Shah Mohammad was forced to abdicate, although the court historian Iskander Beg Munshi says he did this voluntarily: 'The Shah, heavy hearted at the harsh treatment meted out to him by events, sought only peace and security. He demonstrated great joy at meeting his son Abbas and, divesting himself of kingship and royal authority, he placed the crown upon his son's head.'

Steps were now taken to destroy as quickly as possible the powerful enemies who had fallen so easily into the hands of Shah Abbas and Murshid Quli Khan. The following day the leaders whom Abbas distrusted were arrested, and at a formal meeting at the palace:

> the Qizilbash amirs and nobles, standing in serried ranks before the throne, pledged themselves to serve the new Shah loyally. Abbas then accused the amirs of the Abu Taleb faction of being responsible for the murder of his brother Hamza, and demanded their death sentence. All the Qizilbash tribes present signalled their assent. When the accused were brought down from the upper rooms where they had been quartered, they realized what their fate would be. As each entered the hall swords were plunged into them from all sides … the possessions of the executed men were then confiscated.[5]

For more than a year after Shah Mohammad's abdication in October 1588, Abbas, although Shah, was entirely dominated by Murshid Quli Khan, the amir who had brought him from Herat to Qasvin, and who

The young Shah

now, in the role of vizier, took on all important decisions himself. Abbas, though, much resented Murshid's dominant role, and being treated by him as a child. He secretly hated Murshid and only waited until the time was ripe for taking over power for himself. Yet it seems that Murshid was not aware of Abbas's feelings, and continued to make orders in his name without consulting him.

It was the situation in Khorasan that finally led to the fall of Murshid. After he and Abbas had left for Qazvīn the Uzbeks had started a siege of Herat, and Ali Quly Khan, Abbas's former guardian, had been left to defend the city. Abbas repeatedly demanded that Murshid send forces to relieve Herat, but he delayed doing so, being unwilling to help a man who was his enemy and a favourite with the Shah. Eventually, after a year-long siege, Ali Quli Khan was forced to surrender, having been given a promise of safe conduct, but the Uzbeks then broke their word and slaughtered him and the entire garrison. Only then did Murshid organise an army which he himself led towards Herat, accompanied by Abbas, who blamed Murshid for Ali Quly Khan's death and enlisted men he could trust who were prepared to murder him:

> On the night of 23 July [1589], when the army was encamped at Shahrud in the eastern foothills of the Alburz mountains, the Shah detained Murshid Quli Khan in conversation in the royal tent until he fell asleep. He then called in the four assassins, whose turn it was to guard the tent that night, and, after some hesitation, they fell on the sleeping vizier, but failed to kill him outright. Horribly wounded and streaming blood from his throat, he managed to get up and stumble out of the tent, where he was finished off at a signal from the Shah by the keeper of the stables who brought a hammer down on his head.[6]

One of the assassins was Allaverdi Khan, the *ghulam* who later became Abbas's leading general.

This was a turning point in Abbas's reign, and from now on, aged eighteen, he was free to rule as he wanted. There were many immediate challenges to deal with. Various provincial governors were in revolt, and the Ottomans were conducting a new offensive across Persia's western borders. Abbas realised he did not have the power to answer all these threats at the same time so, for the time being, he postponed his campaign against the Uzbeks in Khoristan. Instead, he made a necessary, though humiliating, treaty with the Ottomans which allowed them to keep large swathes of territory they had recently occupied, including the old Persian capital of Tabriz. Then he spent an energetic few months moving his forces round the country putting down revolts in various provinces.

Simultaneously, the Shah started a series of long-term but crucial military reforms designed to reduce the power of the Qizilbash tribes whose rivalries had so weakened the peace and prosperity of the nation in recent years. It was the amirs of these tribes who had frequently refused to obey the orders of the central government to lead their followers into battle. Abbas still needed the Qizilbash to form the main body of his armies, but he wanted to build alternative forces which he could trust and which would owe their allegiance to him rather than to their tribal leaders. This was a Persian version of a process that was also taking place throughout Western Europe at this time. It involved the change from a medieval army made up of feudal levies to a more modern army, paid for and under the control of a central government. This development had already started under Shahs Ismail I and Tahmasp, but Abbas was to take it much further and faster. One method he used, as mentioned in the previous chapter, was the rapid expansion of the corps of *ghulams* (or slave soldiers). These were young men who had been taken from their Christian homes, mainly in Georgia and Armenia, converted to Islam, forcibly or otherwise, and then enlisted and trained in separate regiments. Within a few years the *ghulam* army had increased from a few hundred to between 10 and 15,000. As time went on, Abbas came to trust these *ghulams* and to promote some of them to crucial posts in his administration.

Another element of the Shah's military reforms was to increase the size of the small personal army he had inherited. These soldiers, known as *qurchis*, or household cavalry, consisted of Qizilbash tribesmen who had promised to give up their allegiance to their particular tribe. On recruitment they renounced obedience to their tribal leaders, and instead took a personal oath to the Shah. They were then known as 'lovers of the Shah'. As with the *ghulams,* the *qurchis* could be trusted to do whatever Abbas ordered, and again as with the *ghulams* some rose to high offices previously held by Qizilbash amirs. These new elements of the military were not necessarily stationed in the capital but had their

The young Shah

homes throughout the provinces, and consequently took some time to assemble for a campaign. But they were trained to use the latest weapons available, including muskets instead of the traditional bows and arrows. Abbas also formed an artillery corps equipped with cannon, though this element always remained the weakest in his armies, especially when compared with his Ottoman neighbours.

These reforms, of course, were not popular with the Qizilbash tribes which continued to provide the bulk of the armed forces throughout Abbas's reign. He still needed to keep a watch out for potentially rebellious amirs, and use his considerable diplomatic skills in playing off one powerful tribal leader against another.

The Family of Shah Abbas

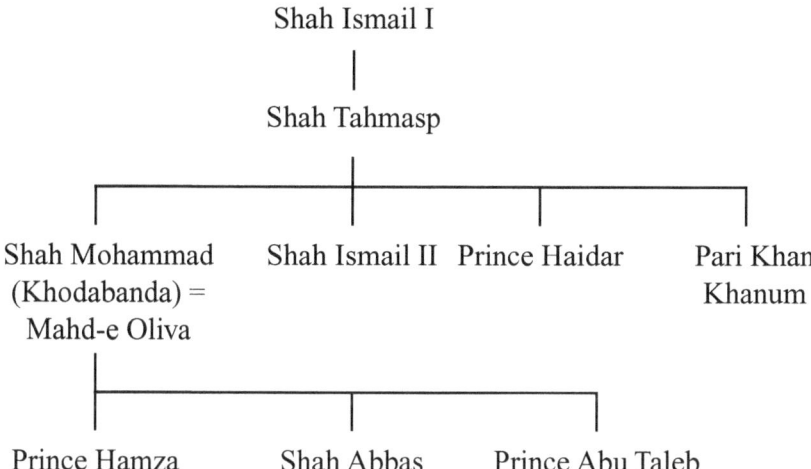

Chapter 9

The nature of Shah Abbas

What kind of man was this Abbas whom Anthony Shirley had travelled so far, and through so many dangers, to meet? The Shah was still young – twenty-seven years old – but already experienced in all the business of kingship, and especially the continuous need to cope with potential enemies, both at home and abroad. He had penetrating greenish eyes, an aquiline nose, and below it long, carefully groomed moustaches which he was very proud of. His head was almost completely shaven, although he was never seen in public without some sort of headgear. He was not particularly tall, but was strongly built and well proportioned. Physically he was very powerful: 'He has extraordinary strength, and with his scimitar can cut a man in two and a sheep with its wool on at a single blow – and the Persian sheep are of a large size,' wrote the Carmelite friar, Fr Paul Simon, who knew him well.[1] The chronicler Iskander Beg Munshi describes a scene at which he was present when, after a battle with the Ottomans, a prisoner 'of huge physical stature' was brought before the Shah. Due to an oversight his hands had not been tied behind his back, as was usual:

> The prisoner suddenly drew a dagger and hurled himself at the Shah. The Shah grabbed his wrist, pulled his arm down and knelt on it. Those near the Shah drew their swords but were afraid to strike because the Shah and his assailant were locked in a fierce struggle and it was difficult to tell which was which, particularly as the prisoner happened to be wearing chain mail and jerkin of the same color as those of the Shah. They stood by helplessly for a considerable time while the Shah grappled with his assailant; finally, the Shah succeeded in wrenching the dagger away from the prisoner's grasp, and the man was seized, dragged away and killed.[2]

The nature of Shah Abbas

As was customary among Persian royalty, Abbas had several wives, two of whom were former Christians, one Georgian and the other from Circassia north of Georgia, a region famed for its beautiful women. Another of his wives was the widow of his murdered elder brother, Hamza. Naturally, too, Abbas had access to any of the women of his harem that he fancied. These women lived in a well-guarded area next to the royal palace, and they might all accompany the Shah when he moved with his court from one part of the country to another. The result of all this was that Abbas had many sons and daughters, legitimate or otherwise. Pietro Della Valle gives us this account of the Shah's behaviour in his harem:

> When he retires to the harem among the women, if he is in a bad mood, no one speaks or goes to him, except for his principal wife, a Georgian and former Christian, who through the great authority she has over him, consoles him little by little, and brings him to a better temper. But when he sometimes relaxes cheerfully, all the women are around him, all speak to him, all joke with him, and, singing and playing, they eat and drink together. And he finds them excellent and numerous company, there being about a hundred all told, very beautiful young women, Georgian for the most part or Circassian, with whom he swaps jokes in great good humour. He is given a tweak by one, and a pull by another, and swept off his feet by his legs, arms and head, to be whirled through the rooms, then thrown down on the carpets, while he calls out: "you strumpets, ah, you mad things."[3]

Nevertheless, Abbas was probably bisexual. Certainly he enjoyed the company of young boys, and provincial governors often sent him presents of boys as well as girls. He was often to be found in coffee houses watching the lascivious dancing of young men, and he was said to be always accompanied by naked boys when he visited the public baths. What we would term pederasty was not uncommon among the upper class of Safavid Persia.

When he was young, Abbas's guardians were careful to give him the best education possible. The fact that he was brought up in Herat, a major cultural centre, meant that they could introduce him to the wide range of arts and crafts practised in the city's workshops, and as an adult he continued to develop the interests and skills he had learnt. According to Fr. John Thaddeus, another Carmelite, who first met the Shah in 1607 and spent several years in Persia: 'He enjoys making scimitars, arquebuses, bridles and saddles for horses, weaving cloth, distilling salts, orange-flower water and medicaments, and – in short – with all mechanical crafts, if not perfect, he is at least somewhat conversant ... unable to remain idle, the King is more intent now on this craft, now on some other occupation, and from the quickness of his nature he will learn it rapidly and do it particularly well.'[4] His special obsession, however, was building. By the time of the Sherleys' visit he had already started to transform the city of Isfahan, which was to be his new capital instead of Qazvīn. During his reign, Isfahan, with its palaces, mosques and gardens, was to become one of the most admired and beautiful cities in the world (see chapter 15).

Abbas enjoyed travelling round his kingdom. He was curious about the lives and occupations of his people, from the lowest to the highest, and he had an aptitude for meeting and conversing with anyone he came across. He liked to visit the stalls in a bazaar, talk to the stall-holders and taste their wares. He saw himself as the friend and ally of all his people. If a peasant or workman were to complain to him about an unjust burden of taxation or the corruption of the local rulers he would immediately summon the official concerned, and if they could not justify their actions, they might even be executed on the spot.

One example of the Shah's willingness to socialise with his people was his patronage of coffee houses. These houses were places of cultural exchange frequented by all the better-off. They were often grand structures with high ceilings: 'Coffee houses in big cities ordinarily had a fountain at their centre and platforms around the walls on which people would sit *À la manière orientale*. They were most crowded in the early mornings and in the evenings. People would pass their time drinking coffee, served with a *hookah* and some tobacco.'[5] The French traveller, Jean Baptiste Tavernier, who visited Isfahan during the reign of Abbas, says that the Shah, 'realizing that people discussed affairs of the realm in the coffeehouse, feared that cabals against the court would be formed.' Consequently, he sponsored mullahs to enter coffeehouses and preach – no doubt to the irritation of many of the guests. 'On occasion he would even enter one himself, and question visitors, just as he did the stall-holders in public markets.'[6] However,

Abbas hated the use of tobacco, and more than once tried to ban it, though without much success.

Coffee is mentioned by both Parry and Manwaring, members of Sherley's party, but both of them in relation to Aleppo rather than Persia. According to Parry, 'the Turks sit upon their stalls, cross-legd for the most part, passing the day in banqueting and carowsing until they surfeit, drinking a certain liquor which they do call Coffe, which is made of a seede much like mustard seede, which will soon intoxicate the braine.'[7] According to Manwaring, 'They have a certain kind of drink which they call koffwey, it is made of an Indian seed; they drink it extremely hot, it is nothing toothsome, nor hath any good smell, but it is very wholesome.'[8]

Coffee houses were a striking element in Persia's urban culture, which predated their arrival in England by a century. Even when coffee started becoming available in England, which was not until the second half of the seventeenth century, it was often regarded with suspicion, as Samuel Chew explains: 'The drink was for a long while regarded as a medicine, a specific against certain diseases; but one to be used with caution because in expert hands it might cause a variety of disorders ranging from vertigo to leprosy. It is not surprising that the demand for it was of slow growth. It was, moreover, costly stuff, not easily obtainable, the taste for it an acquired one, the art of preparing it delectably not easily learnt.'[9]

Another element in the coffee houses, and on the streets of Isfahan, was a pervasive drug culture. According to Kathryn Babayan, 'Isfahani society was geared toward communal socializing and entertainment. Some denizens of Isfahan spent wakeful hours in a state induced by the drinking, eating, or smoking of a variety of drugs, from hashish to opium.' Babayan associates drug users with the unorthodox, but popular, faiths of Sufis and mystics: 'Those who engaged in the drug culture would have been open to the religious orientation of the dervishes, for they would already have had visions of the unseen, experienced a different realm of space and time, and perhaps already sensed the presence of something powerful like God. Drugs were also used, along with music and dance, as a means of attaining a higher state of consciousness or a state of ecstasy.'[10] Clearly, Abbas, with his close links to the mullahs of orthodox Shi'ism, would have been hostile to such ideas, and to the use of drugs (unless, of course, one counts alcohol as a drug!)

Abbas particularly enjoyed talking to foreign visitors. He would question them closely about their own countries, the customs, religion and way of life, and he showed a positive interest even when they were of a different faith from his own. In this he differed markedly from earlier Safavid monarchs. As we have seen, when Abbas's grandfather, Shah Tamasp, was told that the young English merchant, Anthony Jenkinson, was a Christian he was far less tolerant, declaring, 'we have no need to have friendship with the unbelievers.'[11]

As to his personal tastes, Abbas enjoyed ceremonials and displays of every kind, for which he would dress appropriately, but for everyday he preferred a simple costume of red, green or black cloth. His taste in food was also simple, though he enjoyed visiting the royal kitchens and would sometimes cook his own food, especially the game he had caught himself in a hunt. He also drank wine, although this was forbidden under Islamic law. He went in for long hours of drinking with his courtiers or foreign visitors, and he seems to have been able to hold his drink; apparently nobody ever saw him drunk in public. Another recreation was hunting, which he pursued whenever he had a chance and found himself in a suitable place. But royal hunts were far more ambitious affairs than merely leaping on horseback over hedges and ditches in pursuit of a fox: 'In the most common form of hunt, thousands of peasants would be recruited to drive the game for miles around into a large area enclosed by nets, where it was then systematically slaughtered, with the King leading the attack and his courtiers following behind. In one such hunt in 1598 or 1599, Abbas killed 162 gazelles and other animals in the space of a morning.'[12] The Shah was also an excellent rider, and obsessed with anything to do with horses. He spent time in the royal stables, grooming and admiring his own horses, and he much enjoyed playing polo, a sport unknown to Europeans at this time.

As to religion, Abbas firmly supported the mullahs, or senior clergy, of Twelver Shi'ism. This was a logical policy to strengthen the power of the monarchy and the peoples' allegiance. Before Abbas, the years of weak central rule and violence had weakened the loyalty of the Qizilbash tribes towards their Safavid Sufi leader. Now, obedience to the Shah as ordained by God, and as head of the national religion, was substituted for the old reverence to a semi-divine Sufi head. Abbas did all he could to enforce Shi'ism and strengthen links between the clergy and the monarchy. He married five of his six daughters to clerics, built new mosques and theological colleges, especially in his new capital, Isfahan, and poured wealth into maintaining the great Shi'ite shrines at Mashad and Ardabil. For their part, the clergy did their best to help Abbas in declaring that obedience to the Shah was the wish of God. Thus developed the crucial alliance between the religious establishment and the monarch, which was to last until the Islamic revolution of 1978-9, when the mullahs helped overthrow the last Shah of Persia.

In his account of his meeting with Abbas, Anthony Sherley discusses the Shah's own religion. In his typically long-winded style Sherley suggests that Abbas's motives for enforcing orthodox Shi'ism were political, in that he wanted to maintain national unity and oppose the Turks, rather than because of any personal beliefs:

> For the King knowing how potent a uniter of men's minds the self-same religion is for the tranquility of an estate, and the like dis-uniter several religions are for the disturbance of the peace of an estate, he is exceedingly curious and vigilant to suppress through all his dominions, that religion of Mahomet which followeth the interpretation of Uthman and Omar [i.e. Sunnism], and to make his people cleave to that of Ali [i.e. Shi'ism]: not (as I judge) through any conscience, which carrieth him more to the one than the other, but first to extirpate intrinsic factions, then to secure himself the more firmly against the Turks.[13]

However, it seems unduly cynical to argue that Abbas supported Shi'ism only because it suited him as Shah. For one thing, during his reign he made repeated pilgrimages to the sacred shrines at Mashad and Ardabil. His most famous pilgrimage took place a couple of years after the Sherleys' visit: 'Shah Abbas set off from Isfahan on 13 September 1601, while members of his entourage measured the daily distance he covered with a rope. Making stops en route from Isfahan to Mashad, Shah Abbas spent approximately sixty-six days on the journey, which meant he walked about eleven miles a day. He finally arrived in Mashad in the winter. Once there, he engaged in pious activities, participating in religious services and performing various menial tasks at the shrine such as snuffing the candles.'[14] Surely this strenuous hike could not have been undertaken for political reasons alone?

Apart from the Shah's religious convictions, his faith in astrology was also strong, a faith shared by most contemporary rulers, including Queen Elizabeth and Emperor Rudolf II. Abbas had his own court astrologer, Jalal al-din Yazdi, whom he consulted regularly in order to avoid inauspicious occasions. An important example was the claim made by Nuqtavis (an influential Sufi movement) that a Nuqtavi dervish would succeed Abbas as Shah at the start of the coming Moslem year 1002 (27 September 1593). Yazdi confirmed this Nuqtavi forecast, explaining that the conjunction of the two unlucky planets [Saturn and Jupiter] would then fall into the first house of the Shah's horoscope, and so advised him to abdicate for a period of three days during this time, which he duly did. He made a leading Nuqtavi act as Shah, and when the three days were over had him shot. The Nuqtavi movement, which had a strong following in several Persian cities, was then ruthlessly suppressed.'[15]

Abbas's great achievement was to create a well-ordered state and an obedient people, in contrast to the years of chaos that preceded his reign. But to do this he believed that he himself had to be ruthless and cruel, at times quite unnecessarily so, as it seems to us. There are several shocking examples of such cruelty in the accounts of Anthony Sherley's companions. George Manwaring narrates what happened on one occasion when the Shah was displeased with the performance of a mock battle by his soldiers in the main square at Qazvīn:

> Some of his gentlemen being amongst them did not behave themselves to the King's mind; and moreover his soldiers were not so perfect as the King did expect they should; whereupon he presently ran in amongst them with his sword drawn, like to a Herculean offspring, and, upon a sudden, he gave four of them their death's wound. Then did he grow more into blood, and not sparing any, but cut off the arms from divers of them. One gentleman which did but only smile the King never left, and, coming for succour into our company, the King did give him such a blow on the middle, that the one half of his body fell from the other.[16]

Another brutal punishment administered by Abbas himself is described by Abel Pinçon:

> One of his soldiers began laughing and disporting in a garden with a courtesan; she, displeased by the importunity of the soldier, cried out so loudly that the King heard, forthwith had her brought before him and asked her why she called so lustily, to which she replied that he was using force. The soldier was arrested before he had a chance to escape, and was brought into the presence of the King, who with his own hands committed a strange butchery, first of all cutting off, with a knife which he wore, his lips, his nose, his ears, his eyelids and his scalp; he afterwards broke all his teeth with a flint, without this poor unfortunate being able to utter so much as a sigh.[17]

One of Abbas's characteristics noted by all observers was his unpredictability. When he was in a good mood people felt they could joke with him and say anything they liked, but this could change in a moment. According to one observer:

> He will go through the public streets, speak at ease freely with the lower classes, cause his subjects to remain sitting while he himself is standing, or will sit down beside this man and that … accompanying all such condecension he requires that people shall not want in respect towards him, and should anyone fail in this regard, he will punish the individual severely. So the more he demonstrates kindliness to his subjects, and the more familiarly he talks with them, they tremble before him, even the greatest among them, for, while joking, he will have their heads cut off.[18]

Even Iskander Beg Munshi, the court historian who wrote an adulatory account of Abbas's achievements, says that he was 'inclined towards despotic behaviour and had a quick temper'. He gives a chilling example: 'If a father was commanded to slay his son, the order would be obeyed instantly; if the father procrastinated out of compassion, the order would be reversed, and if the son hesitated in his turn another would be sent to put them both to death.'[19]

Cutting off heads seems to have been the usual fate meted out by Abbas's soldiers and servants, either to defeated enemies in time of war, or to accused civilians in peacetime. When the Shah and his army, which had just defeated the Uzbeks in Khorasan, entered the city of Qazvīn, Sherley and his group 'saw such a prospect as is not usually seen, which was, twelve hundred soldiers, horsemen, carrying twelve hundred heads of men on their lances, and some having the ears of men put on strings and hanged about their necks.'[20] The Englishmen might have seen the head of a traitor or two displayed on a stake on London Bridge, but never anything approaching this scale. What might happen to them if they got on the wrong side of this ruthless monarch? It reminds one of the Red Queen in *Alice in Wonderland*: 'the Queen was in a furious passion, and went stamping about, and shouting "Off with his head!" or "Off with her head!" about once a minute. Alice began to feel very uneasy: to be sure, she had not as yet had any dispute with the Queen, but she knew that it might happen any minute, "and then," thought she, "what will become of me? They're dreadfully fond of beheading people here; the great wonder is, that there's anyone left alive!"'

Iskander Beg sums up Abbas's personality as follows:

> The character of the Shah contains some contradictions, for instance, his fiery temper, his imperiousness, his majesty and regal splendour are matched by his mildness, leniency, his ascetic way of life, and his informality. He is equally at home on the dervish's mat and the royal throne. When he is in a good temper, he mixes with the greatest informality with the members of his household, his close friends and retainers and others, and treats them like brothers. In contrast, when he is in a towering rage, his aspect is so terrifying that the same man who, shortly before, was his boon companion and was treated with all the informality of a close friend, dares not speak a word out of turn for fear of being accused of insolence or discourtesy. At such times, the amirs, sultans, and even the court wits and his boon companions keep silent, for fear of the consequences. The Shah, then, possesses these two contrasting natures, each of which is developed to the last degree.[21]

Chapter 10

A meeting

This chapter is about the meeting of our two protagonists – the ruthless Persian monarch and the fearless Elizabethan adventurer. The major source for this meeting is Anthony's own account, entitled *Sir Anthony Sherley His Relation of his Travels into Persia*. There is no means of knowing when he actually wrote this, but it was probably shortly before 1610 when we know he handed over the manuscript to his brother Robert when they met in Spain. Robert took it with him to England and it was printed in 1613, having never been republished since. It has 139 pages, about half of which cover his time in Persia, the rest being about his journeys there and back, and also the recent history of that country.

There are major problems concerning this text. Firstly, it seems to have been written many years after the events described. We can only assume – and hope – that Anthony took detailed notes which he kept with him during his various travels in the years after he left Persia. By the time he wrote he was living in retirement in Granada, and perhaps it is correct to argue that 'an ageing and disappointed man is recalling the great days when he helped, or thought he was helping, to shape the destinies of empires.'[1] Secondly, Anthony gives us the actual words of speeches made at meetings when he was present, but all this must have been passed on to him by his interpreter, Angelo Corrai, perhaps after each session, since he himself did not understand Persian or Turkish. And, thirdly, his motive for writing was clearly not so much to recount his personal adventures as to 'extol the greatness of Shah Abbas and to explain why he was in favour of an alliance with the princes of Christendom.'[2] One might also add that long before he wrote this book Anthony had developed an extremely long-winded and pretentious style, which makes reading it hard work.

Luckily, to supplement Sherley's text the three other accounts written by his followers on their journey (as mentioned in Chapter 6) also cover the time they spent in Persia, and in travelling back to Europe. All three were later published – Pinçon's in French – and they are reproduced by Sir E. Dennison Ross in his 1933 book, *Sir Anthony Sherley and his Persian Adventure*. All three authors do their best to set down what they think will best entertain or surprise their future readers. To give just one example, Parry describes here a system of communication not yet known to Europeans: 'When they desire to hear news or intelligence out of any remote parts of their country with all celerity they have pigeons that are so taught and brought to the hand that they will fly with letters fastened with a string about their bodies under their wings: from whence, if they should send by camels (for so otherwise they must) they should not hear in a quarter of a year, for so long would they be in continual travel.'[3]

On the arrival of Sherley and his party at Qazvīn they were met by the high steward of the Shah's household, who explained that Abbas would shortly be with them and in the meantime had instructed him to provide them with everything they might need. According to George Manwaring, Sir Anthony got off to a good start by impressing this official with his superior status. The steward said, 'In my King's behalf this small kindness I would entreat you to accept in regard of your long and weary travels,' and laid twenty pounds in gold at Sherley's feet.

> But Sir Anthony, accordingly to his princely mind, turning the money over with his foot, returned this answer: "Know this, brave Persian, I come not a begging to thy King, but hearing of his great fame and worthiness thought I could not spend my time better than come to see him, and kiss his hand, with the adventure of my body to second him in his princely wars." The Persian, hearing this answer, stepped back very suddenly, and, making a low *congé,* replied this: "Pardon me, brave stranger, for now I see thou art a Prince thyself, for so it seemeth by thy princely answer."'[4]

Sherley, as we know, regarded himself as a gentleman and a soldier, with little time for unseemly discussions about money (unless he happened to be trying to borrow some from a merchant).

After two or three weeks news came that the Shah and his victorious army were returning home after their successful war against the Uzbeks in Khorasan. However, they halted a few miles from Qazvīn in order to prepare a ceremonial entry into the city. Sherley and his men were told to come and meet Abbas. They saw large crowds lining the route as they awaited his arrival, no doubt with trepidation. But from this first meeting all went well. 'When we came to the King,' reported Anthony, 'we alighted and kissed his Stirrop: My speech was short. I told him that the fame of his Royall vertues had brought me from a farr Countrey. Of what I was, I submitted the consideration to his Majesties judgement, which he should make upon the length, the danger and the expence of my voyage, onely to see him of whom I had received such magnificent and glorious relations.' In reply, Abbas welcomed Anthony and his party, and said that as they had come so far just to see him, they must stay for some time, and get to know him and the country.[5]

The Englishmen were invited to ride beside the king, and they joined the procession which wound its way through the crowds and into the city. There were court officials, horn players and drummers, and serried ranks of cavalry carrying Uzbek heads on their lances. Another feature of the procession noted by Pinçon was 'a large troop of courtesans riding astride in disorder, and shouting and crying in every direction as if they had lost their senses.' These women 'did holloa and gave such a cry, much like the wild Irish,' according to Manwaring.[6] Having reached the main square of Qazvīn the Englishmen were invited to a banquet of rich food, loud music and dancing girls, the first of many such feasts during the coming weeks.

A few days later the Shah invited Anthony to watch him playing polo, a game quite new to the English: 'there was twelve horsemen in all with the King; so they divided themselves six on the one side, and six on the other, having in their hands long rods of wood, about the bigness of a man's finger, and on the end of the rod a piece of wood nailed on like unto a hammer.' A wooden ball was then thrown between the teams, and 'they began their sport, striking the ball with their rods from one to the other, in the fashion of our football play here in England.'[7]

Early on in their acquaintance Anthony was impressed that Abbas seemed less interested in talking 'of our apparell, building, beauty of our women, or such vanities,' as in military matters such as fortifications and artillery. He visited Anthony's apartments and spent three hours looking at 'some books on military science' which Anthony had apparently managed to bring with him all the way from home. When he heard that Anthony himself and most of his companions had fought for their country, and that one of them, Thomas Powell, who became Robert Sherley's friend, was a specialist in gunnery. The Shah was no doubt hopeful that he might receive useful military advice from his new friends.

What is clear throughout all the accounts is the very friendly treatment Anthony Sherley and his group received right from their arrival. According to William Parry, the Shah 'grew more and more into such liking of Sir Anthony that once a day at the least he would send for him to confer, and compliment with him: yea, sometimes he must be sent for to come to his bed-chamber at midnight, accompanied by his brother, for that purpose.'[8] The most likely reason for this friendship is that the group had arrived at just the right moment. The Shah, having decisively defeated the Uzbeks on his eastern border, must have now been contemplating the best moment to declare war against the Turks to the west, who were occupying territory he considered rightfully his. Also, no doubt, he was flattered that a well-connected foreigner, such as Anthony Sherley apparently was, had made such a hazardous long journey in order to meet him.

Anthony himself might have suspected that Abbas was considering an attack on Turkey, but he could hardly be sure. It was perhaps at this point, during his time in Qazvīn, that he changed his own project. Previously, his aims had been focused on trade. He had told the Venetian authorities, and also the English merchants in Aleppo who had given him hospitality, that he was planning to persuade the Shah to set up a new trading route that would bypass the Portuguese in Hormuz. Now, it seems, he came up with a different suggestion which he hoped might attract Abbas more than the issue of trade. The new project was to forge an alliance between Persia and the monarchs of Europe, and attack the Turks from both sides. Whether he was aware of the unsuccessful history of similar schemes, starting as far back as Shah Ismael I and Charles V, is uncertain.

However, Anthony could never be certain what the Shah was really thinking, or what his future plans were. Therefore, for a long time he avoided broaching this new proposal. He wanted first to understand Abbas better, and also get to know the more important courtiers and their attitudes to him, an unknown foreigner, and whether any of them might back his proposed alliance with Christian princes. He knew the dangers of antagonising a ruler like Abbas, especially if that involved going against the king's own views, even when invited to be perfectly honest. He was no doubt aware of Abbas's ruthlessness and cruelty when angered, or if not aware he was shortly to be given a clear illustration, which he recounts in his memoir, although presumably he did not witness it himself.

The governor of Qazvīn, appointed to this important position a few years earlier by Abbas himself, was now accused of corruption and the exploitation of the city's poor for personal gain. Witnesses having been called and the charges proved, the governor was summoned into the royal presence and there sentenced to lose all his goods and land, and to 'goe during his life with a great yoke, like a Hoggesyoke, about his neck, have his Nose and Eares cut off, and have no charitable releefe from any, that he might feel in himselfe the misery which poore men have to get, and what a sinne it is to rent from them by violent extortion.'[9]

After the English group had spent several weeks in Qazvīn, always on excellent terms with the Shah, Abbas announced that he was leaving for his new capital, Isfahan, and invited them to go with him. For their journey he provided them with ready money as well as 'fortie horses all furnished; two with exceeding rich Saddles plated with gold, and set with Rubies, sixteen Moyles [mules], twelve Cammels laden with Tents, and all furniture.' On the journey Anthony felt the time was approaching when he could introduce his Turkish project, and one day, after the Shah had been telling him about the recent relationship between Turkey and Persia, he plucked up the courage to say that 'it was ever almost impossible to preserve a quyet amity betweene two so great Potentates as himselfe and the Turke, especially being so neere neighbours, to which the Shah agreed.'[10]

Shortly after this, Anthony approached Allaverdi Khan, the Shah's leading general, and the courtier whom he gauged was most likely to support his project. Allaverdi Khan had been brought up as a Christian in Georgia before conversion to Islam as a *ghulam*. He had been appointed the leader of the *ghulam* military corps and governor of Shiraz. He was enthusiastic about Anthony's plan to involve the leading European nations, and attack the Turks from both sides. He advised him to propose the scheme to the Shah as soon as possible, though he warned that other courtiers, especially the vizier, Haydar Beg, would strongly oppose it.

When Abbas and his court entered Isfahan, Sherley watched for his chance, and a fortnight later found himself in the palace garden facing the Shah, with only his brother Robert, one other courtier and an interpreter present.[11] Anthony proposed to Abbas that there was nothing more honourable for a prince than to win back what lands had been taken from him by his enemy, that now was the moment to do so, when the Turks were already at war against the emperor in the west, and therefore the time had now come to join with the Christian princes against the common enemy. But he had hardly finished speaking when other courtiers appeared, including the vizier, who immediately set about demolishing his arguments in the course of a long, and obviously prepared, speech.

Haydar Beg said that after the Uzbek campaign Persia was totally unprepared for another war against such a powerful enemy. They lacked the necessary finance, and above all they lacked the siege guns needed to fight the Turks, who, unlike the Uzbeks, held many strongly fortified towns: 'Where is your Majesty's treasure? Where is your munition, and where is your Artillery?' he asked. Then, turning to the Sherley brothers, he said they were adventurers who had been sent 'to disquiet your Maiesties tranquility, and to embark you in dangerous enterprises for others' interests,' and he ridiculed the likelihood that 'a Gentleman of quality should take such a voyage, so full of dangers and expenses, merely upon the fame of a Prince, spread by ordinary Merchants.' He also thought that the whole idea of begging other monarchs for help was demeaning for the king of a great nation like Persia. Haydar Beg finished by suggesting that, instead of attacking Turkey, they should turn their attention to the Portuguese in Hormuz who were making so much profit out of the trade with the East – money that should belong to them. Hormuz, he believed, would be a much easier target. (By a peculiar coincidence this proposal would have fitted in very well with what Anthony had originally told everyone was his purpose in travelling to Persia – to disrupt the Portuguese trade monopoly – but this was before he changed his mind!)

To the arguments of the vizier, Allaverdi Khan replied with a combative speech in Sherley's support: "This Christian,' he said, 'hath come from farre, and through great dangers, through his affection, growing from the excelling fame of his Majesty,' and should not therefore his advice be trusted? As to Persia's lack of munitions and artillery, the solution was to remedy this lack now, and not to defer war until such time as the enemy had made peace in Hungary. And why, he asked, should it demean his majesty 'to invite the Princes Christian to so honourable and great an action?' As for a campaign against the Portuguese in Hormuz, this would entail considerable risk, partly because the territory surrounding that island was barren and inhospitable and could not long support an invading army, and also because they did not have the ships required for such a campaign.

Eventually Abbas put an end to the debate. He himself spoke about the Turkish manner of making war, and about the present condition of the Ottoman Empire, but without appearing convinced by the arguments of either side. Nonetheless, he paid full tribute to Sir Anthony's good faith, and he thanked him for his advice. But the peace party wasted no time, for that very night Haydar Beg and his supporters had another audience with the Shah and seem to have quite won him over, because when Sir Anthony next tried to broach the topic Abbas quickly changed the subject. Nothing more was said on it for the next few weeks, but Anthony got the impression that Allaverdi Khan was out of favour with the Shah.

At this juncture news arrived that the Sultan of Turkey's ambassador, Mohammad Aga, had arrived in Persia with rich presents for Abbas. This seemed a bitter blow for the Sherley party; if the peace between the two nations which Abbas had concluded at the start of his reign was now to be renewed, it would mean not only the end of Anthony's project, but perhaps also the end of their entire Persian mission. All this caused Anthony so much stress that he became seriously ill, and took to his bed for several days: 'it did so exceedingly fill my very soule with perplexitie and anxietie that I fell into a very dangerous sicknesse.' During this time the Shah used to visit him, and 'finding that the recordation of those things did aggravate both the griefe of my minde and unquiet of my bodie, he forbad that any in my presence should speake more of it.'[12]

At length Mohammad Aga reached Isfahan, and after a few days rest, had his audience with Abbas. Anthony was then still unwell, so Robert went in his stead. It turned out that the Turkish ambassador had totally misjudged the situation. His speech was highly demanding, and given in a very superior and patronising manner. After a long harangue about the might and power of his master, Sultan Mohammed III, he informed Abbas that 'he was sent to admonish him to remain constant in the truce with his Master,' and that his master demanded the restitution of Khorasan to the former Uzbek governmnent, and also the return of 10,000 Kurds who had recently fled from Turkish territory and been given permission to stay in Persia. If Abbas complied with these terms, then his master might consider renewing the peace; if not, there would be consequences.

Finally, he also demanded that the Shah send his eldest son, Prince Safi, to Constantinople as a hostage to ensure compliance.

Abbas, thrown into a fury at Mohammad Aga's speech, now ordered that the ambassador's beard be shaved off and sent to the Sultan with the suggestion that he should eat it. Such insults were known to be common at the time between these two nations. A Persian historian remembers an earlier insult to an ambassador, only this time by a Turkish sultan to a Persian Shah: 'Shah Abbas was indeed within his right to do it, in order that Sultan Mohammad should recall to mind the trick played by order of his father, Murad III, on a former Persian ambassador, who, during certain solemn ceremonies at the court of Constantinople, was put to stand upon a flooring, traitorously set, then ignominiously to be thrown down beneath the same at the most important moment of that ceremony.'[13]

Naturally, the effect of Mohammad Aga's speech was to antagonise the Shah and his subjects all the more against the Turks, and to drive waverers into the belief that a warlike policy was justified. The next day the Shah came to see Sir Anthony, who was still convalescing from his illness. He told him that he had decided to send an ambassador to the monarchs of Europe and try to enlist them in a joint war against the Turks. He wanted Sherley to be that ambassador: 'because you have been the Mover and Persuader of this business, you shall also be the actor of it, assuring myself that my honour cannot be more securely reposed in any man's hands.'[14] This offer was, of course, enthusiastically accepted, although Sir Anthony asked that a Persian nobleman should go with him, to which Abbas agreed. In this way Mohammad Aga did Sherley's work for him, and made his dream come true.

There followed a month of feasting and relaxation at the Shah's court while preparations for the embassy were made. Sir Anthony was to pick who were to receive the letters, and his choice fell on the following: the Emperor Rudolf II (who was already fighting the Turks in Hungary), the Pope, Queen Elizabeth, Henry IV of France, Philip III of Spain, the Senate of Venice, the Grand Duke of Tuscany, James VI of Scotland and, last but not least in Sherley's eyes, the Earl of Essex. The Shah included in each letter that European merchants would be allowed trade with Persia without paying taxes or custom duties, and there would be complete toleration for visiting Christian merchants to pursue their religion. Meanwhile, the choice had to be made as to who was to go

A meeting

on this new embassy. There were to be about twenty-four persons, not including servants. Of those Englishmen who had come to Persia six months earlier, at least seven were chosen, including, of course, Sir Anthony himself. But his eighteen-year-old brother, Robert, was left behind, perhaps as a kind of guarantee that Anthony would return to collect him after the mission was over. Abbas promised to treat him as his own son, and there is no evidence that Robert was unhappy at this decision. The Persian nobleman chosen was Hussein Ali Beg, a senior courtier of dignified appearance.

Shortly before the expedition was due to set out from Ispahan an unexpected event occurred. An Augustinian friar, Nicholas de Melo, arrived from Hormuz, and asked Sir Anthony to obtain an audience for him with the Shah. Melo claimed to be Bishop of Hormuz and a relation of the late king of Portugal, and when he heard about Sir Anthony's mission to Europe, expressed an interest in joining it. Sir Anthony was no doubt impressed with his credentials, but at the audience with Abbas, 'there in my own presence, he desired the King to put no confidence in me.' In spite of this curious behaviour, the two became reconciled, and Sherley obtained for de Melo permission to accompany the others, and also from the Shah 'a particular letter both to the Pope and King of Spain in which he should have equal authority with me.' But the friar's presence on the expedition was a harbinger of future difficulties to come.

Chapter 11

Travelling as an ambassador

In May 1599, a large group led by Sir Anthony Sherley left Ispahan intending to journey to Europe via the Caspian Sea and Russia. They included English and Persians, diplomats and adventurers, interpreters and servants: 'There were withal thirty-two camels carrying the presents [for foreign rulers] besides the needful number of riding horses for those who went the journey, and the usual sumpter-beasts required for carrying the baggage of the various persons.'[1] They knew they could not take the shortest route through Turkey because by now the Turkish authorities were fully aware that Sherley and the others were not merchants as they had once pretended to be, and also they probably knew all about the plan to form an anti-Turkish alliance between Shah Abbas and Christian princes.

During the return from Persia to Europe Anthony Sherley continued his account of events, and so did his three companions, Parry, Manwaring and Pinçon, but on this journey they were joined by yet another voice, a Persian who later converted to Catholicism, changed his name to Don Juan, and published his account under his new name when living in Spain. Don Juan makes several important points not mentioned by the others. One is that when Sherley first arrived in Qazvīn 'he gave himself out as cousin of the Scottish King James, saying that all the Kings of Christendom had recognized him as such, and had now empowered him as their ambassador to treat with the King of Persia.'[2]

This was the high point of Anthony's entire career. He had formed his latest project either during his journey to Persia, or possibly when he was in Qazvīn. He had led his followers through numerous dangers until they arrived, as penniless adventurers, at the Persian court. Now he was an honoured ambassador, despatched to broker a grand anti-Ottoman alliance between the Shah of Persia and the monarchs of Europe. News of his achievements was already starting to reach England, as is shown by a letter to him from Sir Francis Vere.

Vere was perhaps his country's most admired soldier, and had commanded the English army fighting against the Spanish in the Netherlands, which is no doubt where Sherley had first got to know him. Writing 'To my good friend Sir Anthony Sherley,' Vere expresses his admiration for Anthony's achievements in Persia, and his envy of what he was doing: 'Yet this envye of myne shall not be so wicked as to make me wyshe from you any thing, but rather that I myght be partaker with you in the experyence to be gathered in these great actiones, and in doing service to so worthye a Prynce [i.e. Shah Abbas], who hath no small reverence amongst men of any profession for whatsoever he doeth to Noble Sir Anthony.'[3] Unfortunately, like other letters to Sherley from England, this one was seized by government agents and never reached him, which is why it is to be found today among the Cecil Papers at Hatfield (see Appendix III).

The ambassadorial party wound its way northwards to the shores of the Caspian Sea where they had to wait several weeks for Hussein Ali Beg, the Persian nobleman chosen to accompany them, to catch up. Then they took ship, but their voyage turned out to be long and perilous. Abel Pinçon was highly critical of the crew of their ship. 'Our sailors,' he remarked, 'are ill-versed in their trade, for they understand as much about the stars as pigs do about spices, and they never use the compass: that is the reason why they always keep close inshore, not daring to venture into the open sea.' In spite of this caution they were subject to frightening storms, and Pinçon describes one particular day when they all thought their end had come: 'One heard a dreadful medley of voices and prayers. We of the Religion prayed in one way; there were some Portuguese monks who threw figures of the Agnus Dei into the sea to appease it, and muttered certain words, repeating Virgin Mary, St John and the In Manus. The Mahommedans invoked Ali, Ali Mahomet, but instead of all these I feared that the Devil would come to carry this rabble to Hell. But when we had been three hours in this storm God cast on us His eye of pity and delivered us.'[4]

After two months at sea they reached the mouth of the Volga and met with a party of Russian soldiers who were expecting them. The soldiers rowed the party upstream to Astrakhan where they stayed a fortnight while the governor of the city sent a messenger to Moscow to ask the Czar how to treat them. Then they were provided with transport, food and escorts for the long journey, first up the Volga and then, when the river was frozen, by sled to Novgorod, arriving finally in Moscow sometime in September.

During all these months of travel there was plenty of time for the various factions and individuals within the party to quarrel with each other, and in particular Melo, the Augustinian friar, with Sir Anthony. It seems that early in the journey Melo had admitted he was not what he had claimed to be: 'In a gamesome vein he further confessed how he would bring men's wives, after he had shriven them, to his bent, as taking advantage of their confessed faults, and also that when staying in Sir Anthony's house in Isfahan he had found the means to have a Persian courtesan to lie with him, and so had night after night during his continuance there.'[5] He also admitted that the present he had given Shah Abbas when he first arrived in Isfahan was actually not from him at all but from the Portuguese governor of Hormuz. All this enraged Sir Anthony, and he had Melo kept as a prisoner for much of the journey. In a letter about the Melo affair written a few months later, he wrote, 'his behaviour was such that for male and female of all sorts I think under heaven there lives not such a villain.'[6]

In Moscow Sir Anthony was annoyed to discover that the Czar (Boris Godunov), having read the various letters from the Shah which the group had brought with them, had decided that Husein Ali Beg, and possibly also Melo, were the true ambassadors, but that he himself was merely a traveller passing through Russia, and in fact very possibly a spy. The fault here lay with Shah Abbas, who, by appointing two ambassadors, neither with precedence over the other, had inevitably stored up future trouble. On this point the 'letters of credence' which Abbas had written to the various European monarchs about Sir Anthony and Ali Beg were vaguely worded, perhaps deliberately so. For instance, Abbas had written to the Emperor Rudolf, 'Valorous Sir Anthony Sherley came to Persia from Frankland. He has enjoyed the highest rank in our service. An honoured subject of ours goes with him as Ambassador to the sovereigns. We desire that you should treat with the said Sir Anthony and consider him as our supreme commissioner.'[7] Who then was to be considered higher, an ambassador or a supreme commissioner?

After several days of confinement for the whole group, Sir Anthony and Melo found themselves brought before a Russian tribunal for interrogation. Sherley haughtily refused to enter the room behind the Persians, arguing that it was the height of indignity for a Christian to walk behind pagans. During their interview de Melo accused Sherley of stealing 1,000 crowns and ninety diamonds from him, while Sherley accused the friar of sodomising two of his attendants. 'Whereupon Sir Anthony, being inflamed with choler, he, not able, though instantly he should have died for it, to suppress his heat, gave the fat friar such a sound box on the face that down falls the friar, as if he had been struck with a thunderbolt.'[8] Amazingly, when he was told what had happened, the Czar was so impressed with this display of force that he decided to free them all from close confinement, except Melo who remained a prisoner. Later, Sir Anthony discovered that Melo had been secretly celebrating mass for some Catholics who lived in Moscow and was able to use this information to get him banished to a remote Russian monastery, and out of his way.

More important than the quarrel with Melo was that other dispute between Sir Anthony and Ali Beg as to which of them was the real ambassador to the princes of Europe. The Czar continued to treat the Persian as the true ambassador, and he also refused to allow the group to leave Moscow, keeping them under permanent observation. Sir Anthony became increasingly depressed as he saw his chances of fulfilling his mission slipping away. In a letter to Anthony Bacon, Essex's secretary, he wrote: 'Hither I came to Russia in September and now it is February, and am yet held prisoner myself, and that which is most of all, none of my Countrymen suffered to come unto me.'[9]

At the conclusion of this long letter, in which he recounted the whole story of Melo, he spoke about his loss of honour, and begged Bacon or Essex to write back comforting him: 'O that I might place myself with one hour to talk with my Lord or you, or both, but since I am so unhappy that I cannot, for God's sake be not negligent in comforting me, and strengthening me to my business, for I protest unto you I am exceeding faint. For that unseen thing called honour is so hourly before my mind that by Jesus I am divided from myself by not knowing what to determine upon.'[10]

At about Easter 1600, after an enforced stay of over six months, the group were finally allowed to leave Moscow, and they continued their journey towards Archangel on the White Sea, then the main port for Russia. The Persian who was later called Don Juan describes the city:

> The population of Archangel, to my judgment, is about 12,000 householders, or 54,000 souls; it is a very famous port, where the French, English and German ships having

commerce with the northern regions of Asia discharge their cargoes. There is here a great breakwater, which covers the entrance to the port; and this last faces south, being very spacious and safe where vessels may anchor. Very often there are as many as 400 ships lying in this harbour, and the customs levied here bring in a good revenue to the Duke of Muscovy. We stayed twenty days in Archangel, getting through our business, and finally made arrangements to embark in a Flemish ship of a thousand tons burden, chartered to sail from this port and well armed, having twenty pieces of cannon.[11]

Meanwhile, the old quarrel between Sir Anthony and Ali Beg, went on unabated. While the two were in Archangel waiting for a suitable ship for the next part of their journey, there occurred the affair of the Shah's presents for the European princes. These were in thirty-two cases. Don Juan describes Sherley's account of what happened:

> When, therefore, we were now about to embark on our sea voyage, Sir Anthony told us that it would be much safer not to carry the great cases containing our presents for the various Christian sovereigns with us in the Flemish ship, seeing that she was an old vessel and not of burden to bear such heavy goods. And further, that if we should encounter bad weather, and that they should have to lighten the ship by throwing cargo overboard, the cases with our presents would infallibly be the first to go. Then he told us that he had a great friend in Archangel, an Englishman, who was master of a very fine stout ship, and that he would take charge of our cases, and deliver them to us again safely when we got to Rome. All this, therefore, appearing to us trustworthy and reasonable, we consigned our great chests to this Englishman, as Sir Anthony had advised us.[12]

The cases were supposed to be delivered in Rome by Sir Anthony's friendly captain, but they never turned up. Apparently, when asked later to account for their disappearance, Sir Anthony produced a different explanation. He said that when he examined the cases in Archangel

Wiston, West Sussex, the home where the Sherley brothers were brought up. (Wikimedia Commons)

Anthony Sherley, aged 23, when he was a captain fighting in the Netherlands under the Earl of Leicester. See Appendix IV. (Wikimedia Commons)

Anthony Sherley, aged about 38. (Dominicus Custos, Prague: Wikimedia Commons)

Robert Sherley, painted in Rome when visiting Pope Paul V in 1616. (Unknown artist: Wikimedia Commons)

Double portrait of Robert Sherley and Teresia Sampsonia, c.1627. (R.J. Berkeley collection: Wikimedia Commons)

Shah Ismail I of Persia (1487-1524). (Uffizi Gallery, Florence: Wikimedia Commons)

Shah Tahmasp I (1524-1576). (Uffizi Gallery, Florence: Wikimedia Commons)

Shah Abbas I (1588-1629. (Dominicus Custos: Wikimedia Commons)

The wild side of Shah Abbas, caught by an unknown Italian artist. (Caroline Mawer: Wikimedia Commons)

Shah Abbas with a page, perhaps revealing his well-known attraction towards young boys. (Wikimedia Commons)

Allaverdi Khan Bridge (Bridge of Julfa), Isfahan. (Eugène Flandin, 1851: Wikimedia Commons)

Royal Square (Jahan Square), Isfahan, built by Shah Abbas. (Wikimedia Commons)

A covered souk in Aleppo. (Graham van der Wielen: Wikimedia Commons)

Persians carrying Turkish heads after the reconquest of Tabriz in 1603. (Wikimedia Commons)

Hussein Ali Beg, Anthony Sherley's rival ambassador in 1599. (Egidius Sadeler, Prague, 1601: Wikimedia Commons)

Boris Godunov, the Russian Czar who held Anthony and his party in Moscow for six months. (Wikimedia Commons)

The Pitti Palace, Florence, where Anthony was staying when he heard the news that his patron, Essex, had been executed. (Wikimedia Commons)

Robert Dudley, Earl of Leicester, under whom Anthony Sherley served as a captain in the Netherlands. (Unknown artist, Yale Center for British Art: Wikimedia Commons)

Robert Devereux, 2nd Earl of Essex, and Anthony Sherley's patron. (Marcus Gheeraerts the Younger: Wikimedia Commons)

Marino Grimani, Doge of Venice, receiving Persian ambassadors, early 17th century. (Wikipedia Commons)

Gaspar de Guzman, Duke of Olivares. It was Olivares to whom Sherley dedicated his book, *Peso Politico* in 1622. (Velázquez, Hermitage Museum, St Petersburg: Wikimedia Commons)

Emperor Rudolf II (1576-1612) who sent Anthony Sherley to Morocco. (Hans von Aachen, Kunsthistorisches Museum, Vienna: Wikimedia Commons)

James I of England, who favoured the Sherley family. (Kunsthistorisches Museum, Vienna: Wikimedia Commons)

Henry IV of France who knighted Anthony Sherley in 1593. (Jacques Boulbène, Musée des Carmelites: Wikimedia Commons)

Edward Denison Ross, 1856-1941, founder of SOAS, University of London, and author of *Sir Anthony Sherley and his Persian Adventure* (John Lavery: Wikimedia Commons)

he found that the gifts 'were of very little value; indeed, instead of being worth 300,000 crowns as invoiced, 3,000 was their limit. He had therefore sent them all back to Persia as being entirely unsuitable for presentation to the European potentates by an ambassador, a personage of his degree.'[13] To sum up, it does seem likely that Sir Anthony sold the gifts to his naval friend in Archangel, although such an action seems odd, considering that their disappearance was bound to be noticed sooner or later and would merely provide more ammunition to his rival, Ali Beg. Perhaps the affair is an indication that he was mentally adrift due to the stress and worry of the journey.

In June 1600, they sailed from Archangel, rounded Norway and Denmark, and landed, first at Stade on the Elbe, and then at Emden near the border between Germany and Holland. Off Emden one of the group, William Parry, transferred to a passing merchant ship bound for England, taking with him Sir Anthony's letters written at Archangel. Among these were emotional letters to Robert Cecil and the Queen in which he acknowledged his fault in leaving England without permission two years earlier, and asked to be allowed to come home. He declared that the light in the eyes of Queen Elizabeth were for him 'the fairest light in the world', and that all his adventures had only been to 'do some extraordinary thing which might honour Her Majesty's most excellent person and bring generall profitt to my Country'. He begged Cecil to intercede on his behalf with Elizabeth, describing himself as 'a withered branch cut off from any hope of good.'[14]

However, he was soon to discover that his plea would be ignored. His request to return to England was immediately refused, as we know from a letter, dated October 1600, from Cecil to Henry Lello, the English ambassador at Constantinople, which brought Lello up to date with Sherley's actions and the Queen's attitude to him:

> Because I doubt not but you may have heard, as well of Sir Anthony Sherley's returne into these parts as you dyd of his passage into Persia, I have thought good to make you acquainted with that which is true ... First, you must know that he went out of this countrey without any manner of allowance from her Majesty, neither was she ever, since his departure, consenting to any purpose or project of his ... On his arrival in Persia he wrote many letters insinuating

> that he himself was of so great credit with [Shah Abbas], as he could undertake to settle great security and commodity to our merchants. Her Majesty did foresee how dangerous it might have been to her merchants trade with the Grand Seigneur [the Turkish Sultan] if any such practics should have been set on foot ... Now he hath taken the audacity to write to the Queen, assuring her that he would bring her from the Persian a grant of all privileges and immunities for her subjects if they would trade there, and to that end desired liberty to come unto her. Hereupon Her Majesty hath increased her former displeasure towards him so far, in respect of this presumption, as by no meanes she will suffer him to come into the Kingdome.[15]

Parry also carried to England a letter from Sherley to Essex. By the time this was written, Sir Anthony must have known that his patron was in deep trouble, having returned from a disastrous military campaign in Ireland only to be put under house arrest (see Chapter 13). He wrote, 'I am plunged in grief to hear of your Lordship's misfortunes, but my devotion to you is as great as ever.' His world was starting to disintegrate, because the only person capable of arranging his honourable return to England was becoming incapable of doing so.

Apart from Parry, the rest travelled slowly across Germany in hired coaches, receiving hospitality from various German princes along the route. In October they arrived at Prague, the capital of the Holy Roman Emperor, Rudolf II, where they were received with imposing ceremony. Rudolf, whose armies had already spent years fighting against the Turks, seemed very receptive to Sherley's plans for an anti-Turkish alliance with Persia, and promised he would do all he could to further the project (though in fact the time it took for messages to pass between Prague and Ispahan made this whole scheme quite unrealistic, and it never came about). They stayed in Prague for three months, enjoying royal hospitality, until the time came to move on. The plan was to proceed to Venice, but this was refused by the Venetians who had been warned about Sherley's project and – like Queen Elizabeth – were strongly opposed to anything that would disrupt their relations with Turkey, a major trading partner.

Leaving Prague, Sherley's group crossed the Alps and made a brief visit to Florence, arriving in March 1601. They met the Grand Duke

Ferdinand, and were lodged in the Pitti Palace, being treated with great favour. In Florence Sir Anthony also met an old acquaintance, and relative by marriage, Sir Henry Wotton, whose career he now assisted by introducing him to Duke Ferdinand. Later that year Ferdinand sent Wotton to Scotland to warn James about a Spanish plot on his life, and this put him in permanent favour with the future king of England.[16]

But it was during his stay in Florence that Anthony heard the terrible news that the Earl of Essex had been found guilty of treason and executed. He had lost the person he most admired in the whole world. It was the turning point of his entire life and career, and it must have been now that he first thought of switching allegiance to another master and another nation. We know that early in 1601, having left Florence for Rome, Sherley met the Spanish ambassador and gave him advice on how the Spanish might invade and conquer England. He discussed the best places for landing, and chose Sandwich which, he said, could soon be rendered impregnable to counter-attack, and from where the landing force could strike at London. The capital could then easily be taken by twelve or fifteen hundred men, since, 'It is common knowledge that the city of London is entirely alienated from the Queen, because of the death of the Count of Essex.'[17]

In Rome the party enjoyed another magnificent reception. Pope Clement VIII had looked forward to meeting Ali Beg and Sherley since he already knew about their mission, and had been given, by Angelo Corrai and others, highly exaggerated information that Persia might be ripe for conversion to Christianity. But on the way to Rome the quarrel between the two ambassadors intensified. They argued over precedence, and over Ali Beg's accusation that Sherley had stolen all the gifts intended for Christian monarchs. When they reached the palace where they were to stay, they scuffled on the staircase over who should have the better apartment. 'Perhaps someone may be found,' wrote the French ambassador in Rome, 'who shall tell them that since they being but two, and sent by the same prince on the same mission, cannot agree between themselves, they will find it difficult to bring about a union of so many Christian princes and others in order to ruin the empire of the Turk.'[18] The Pope did his best to arrange a reconciliation between the two, but eventually decided to give them separate audiences, much of which each spent in attacking the other. But they did both agree that Shah Abbas wanted to have Catholic missionaries sent to Persia, which much pleased the Pope.

After a few weeks in Rome, mainly spent in quarrels between the Persians and the English, the joint mission sent by Shah Abbas finally broke up. Ali Beg decided to continue the mission by travelling to Spain to give another of the Shah's letters to King Philip III. He did deliver the letter, but then died on his way home to Persia. Sherley, on the other hand, seems to have entirely abandoned his role as Persian ambassador. He suddenly quitted Rome at the end of May 1601, leaving unpaid debts behind, and without telling even members of his own party where he was going. He travelled southwards, down the Adriatic to Ragusa, from where he was probably planning to return to Persia via Turkey disguised as a merchant. If so, he gave up this scheme when he received news that one of his servants in Rome had stolen his copies of letters between Emperor Rudolf and Shah Abbas, which had then been passed to the Turkish government. This would have meant certain arrest for Sir Anthony if he had set foot on Turkish soil.

Chapter 12

Opinion at home

This chapter is about what people in England thought about the Islamic world during the second half of Elizabeth's reign, and how the story of the three Sherley brothers contributed to such opinions. It turns out that English public opinion was at odds with the policies of the Elizabethan government, especially when it came to relations with Turkey.[1]

From the 1570s, as English merchants developed trade links, first with Morocco and then with Turkey, there was increasing interest in the Islamic world. A few people of colour, black or brown, actually visited England, and some could occasionally be seen in public. For instance, Mohammad al Annuri, an ambassador from the king of Morocco, arrived in London in August 1600 with a large delegation to propose an Anglo-Moroccan alliance against the common enemy, Spain. Nothing came of this scheme, but the ambassador visited the Queen twice, and his appearance evoked great interest in court circles.

Very few Englishmen knew much about Moslem culture from which Annuri came. They tended to class all those whose skin was different from their own as Moors, Turks or 'Mahometans', and saw them generally as exotic, and possibly threatening, beings from another world. Descriptions of this unknown world in books written by travellers (or armchair travellers) fulfilled what has been called the 'appetite for the wonderful' shown by 'civilized Englishmen'. If an author wanted to describe life in Turkey, for example, he was expected to titillate his readers with anecdotes about the outrageous, the sensual, the cruel, the deviant, so that they could feel secure in their own moral and political sphere.

One example of such titillation, which lacks a firm evidential basis, was sodomy. As one historian points out, 'There are no texts [in this period] that place homosexuality in English cultural history, while nearly every text on the Moslem dominions does – even if it is anecdotal and brief.'[2] Take the book about his time in Turkey written by Sir Thomas Sherley, elder brother of Sir Anthony, when he finally returned home in 1607.

(Admittedly, he had much to resent about his treatment after he had been a prisoner of the Turks – see Chapter 5): 'Theyre mannor of living in private and in general is most uncivil and vicious; and first, for their vices they are all pagans and infidels, sodomites, liars and drunkards, and for their soddommarye they use it so publically and impudently as an honest Christian would shame to company with his wife as they do with their buggering boys.'[3]

From when the first London commercial playhouses opened in 1576 until the end of Elizabeth's reign it has been estimated that over sixty plays included an actor playing a Turk, a Moor or a Persian, and of these, forty were staged during the last decade of the reign.[4] Most show these characters as unpredictable outsiders, fascinating but dangerous. However, the most famous of them, Shakespeare's Othello, reveals a more ambiguous and complex figure, a black 'Moor' who has risen to power in the Christian world of Venice. Yet even Othello might have been recognised by Elizabethan audiences as someone who, at the end of the play, exposes his real nature and 'turns Turk' by murdering his innocent wife and then himself.

Shakespeare wrote *The Tragedy of Othello, the Moor of Venice* in about 1601, although it was not staged until three years later, but the story of race in Elizabethan England ends with the proclamation of 1601 which, at a time of economic distress caused by a succession of weak harvests, put some of the blame on 'negroes and blackamoors' as opposed to the Queen's 'own natural subjects'. The reasons given for wanting to expel such people have a curiously modern ring: that they do not sympathise with our culture and religion, that there are too many of them, and that money is wasted looking after them

> Whereas the Queen's majesty, tendering the good and welfare of her own natural subjects, greatly distressed in these hard times of dearth, is highly discontented to understand the great number of negroes and blackamoors which (as she is informed) are carried into this realm since the troubles between her highness and the King of Spain, who are fostered and powered here, to the great annoyance of her own liege people who covet the relief which these people consume, as also for that the most of them are infidels having no understanding of Christ or his Gospel: hath given

a special commandment that the said kind of people shall be with all speed avoided and discharged out of this her majesty's realms.[5]

This proclamation shows the Elizabethan government attempting to pander to public opinion in difficult times by focusing on a tiny but conspicuous and unpopular minority. It may have been especially aimed at those North Africans who had accompanied the Moroccan ambassador Annuri to England, but, as mentioned above, most English hardly distinguished between Moroccans and other people of colour. In particular, Turks were feared and hated because their nation seemed to threaten the very existence of the civilized West.

The Ottoman Empire, stretching from the Black Sea to Egypt, was the greatest power in the known world, and everyone had heard about how it had swallowed up Hungary and reached the gates of Vienna under its famous sultan, Suleiman the Magnificent. They knew, too, about the success and brutality of the Barbary pirates who, with support from Constantinople, preyed on the merchant shipping of all nations, and forced hundreds of captured Englishmen to become their galley slaves. The terrible story of how, on the death of Sultan Murad in 1595, his successor, Mehmed, had his nineteen brothers put to death was also common knowledge, and must have confirmed popular belief in Turkish brutality: 'They say [wrote the Venetian ambassador in Constantinople] that the eldest, a most beautiful lad and of excellent parts, beloved by all, when he kissed the Sultan's hand exclaimed, "My lord and brother, now to me as my father, let not my days be ended thus in this my tender age." The Sultan tore his beard with every sign of grief, but answered never a word. They were all strangled.'[6]

To sum up, by the time the Sherley brothers reached Persia there was, and had been for years, a powerful anti-Turk sentiment in England.

This popular feeling, however, was contradicted by the policies of Elizabeth's government. Since the beginning of Elizabeth's reign, and especially after 1570, when Pope Pius V excommunicated the Queen for 'having seized on the Kingdom and monstrously usurped the place of Supreme Head of the Church in all England,' the country had found itself more and more isolated in Europe. One result of this was that the government encouraged English merchants to develop new trade in places outside the control of Catholic powers, particularly Spain. This led to close links, firstly with Morocco – hence the visit of Annuri – and then with Turkey. Morocco supplied England for the first time with sugar and candied fruit (leading to the blackness and decay of Elizabeth's teeth), but the overall potential for Moroccan trade was small compared to the profitable trade with Ottoman Turkey which developed during the 1580s.

In 1578 an important 'Memorandum on the Turkey trade' by Francis Walsingham, Elizabeth's principal secretary, suggested that developing direct trade between England and Turkey would cut out middle men such as the Venetians, and produce large profits. To create this new trade would not be easy because it involved rivalry with Spain and France as well as Venice, all of whom already traded with the Turks, had their own agents in Constantinople, and would oppose Protestant England's arrival on the scene. Walsingham suggested the solution was 'to make choice of some apt man to be sent with her Majesty's letters unto the Turk to procure an ample safe-conduct, who is always to remain there at the charge of the merchants.' It proved an acceptable plan, both to Elizabeth who would save money, and to potential merchants who would have royal support for this untried new venture. Merchants wanting to trade with Turkey would be bonded together in a joint-stock company. This recently invented business model made it easier to raise capital, while reducing the risk for individual merchants.

The 'apt man' chosen to represent the new company in Turkey was William Harborne, a resourceful and much-travelled merchant who had already worked for the government as a spy. Constantinople was a vast cosmopolitan city, far larger than any cities in the West, with people from many nations living together, but it was virgin territory for the English when Harborne arrived. Over the next few years he was to successfully overcome many problems – not just the jealousy of other foreign agents, but also language issues plus the difficulty of ever actually getting to meet with the Sultan (known as the Grand Turk) due to the complexities of the opaque Turkish bureaucracy.

At this time a struggle for power was going on between the royal harem, dominated by Murad's consort, Safiye Sultan, and the grand vizier, Sokollu Mehmed. Harborne managed to make friends with the vizier, who in turn persuaded Sultan Murad to correspond with Elizabeth, and eventually to grant the English full commercial rights throughout Ottoman lands. All this was not achieved without frequent expensive gifts for the Grand Turk, chosen personally by the Queen. For instance, in 1599 Elizabeth sent the new Sultan, Mehmet, a coach worth £600 together with 'an organ very cunningly designed, which serves as a clock and can play several tunes by itself.'[7]

Within a few years Harborne had installed a network of English agents across the Turkish empire, including in Aleppo, Damascus, Cairo and islands in the Aegean. The joint stock company, now named the Levant Company, and with over fifty members, was making exceptional profits on a wide exchange of goods. Their exports to Turkey were primarily woollen cloth and various metals including lead, and also broken bell metal from the bells of Catholic monasteries and chantries dissolved at the Reformation. Imports included silk, cotton, and carpets as well as diamonds, pearls and sapphires. Soon at least five convoys of English ships were making their way to Turkish ports every year.

From time to time voices were raised against this new trade with the enemies of the Christian religion. Soon after it started, the bishop of London, John Aylmer, sent a letter to the Lord Mayor of that city asking if the trade could somehow be stopped. One of his concerns was for English sailors who had been captured and placed in Turkish galleys, seemingly without protest from English merchants trading with Turkey. 'If your Lordship and the rest of your brethren,' he wrote, 'could by your authority stay such intercourse with infidels and save the souls of our people from the Gulf of Mahomet, I think you should do a gracious deed and win an everlasting remembrance.'[8] Popular sentiment may well have been on the side of the bishop, but this was a trade that neither the Elizabethan government nor the powerful merchants of the city of London would allow to be threatened in any way. A good example of official sensitivity to potential troublemakers was what happened some years later to Sir Thomas Sherley when he found himself under interrogation in the Tower of London for proclaiming his view that the trade with Turkey was 'abominable & naughte'. (See the end of Chapter 5.) And before this, as we know, his brother Anthony had been in trouble for suggesting an alliance of nations against Turkey.

We now turn back to Anthony, and the way his story was presented to the English public in a series of publications, and also in a play produced on the London stage. During the first decade of the seventeenth century the adventures of Sir Anthony Sherley in Islamic lands became widely known in England. To start with, two booklets were produced during

1600-01 by members of the group that had accompanied Sir Anthony on his Persian expedition. The first of these was an anonymous pamphlet printed in 1600, entitled *A True Report of Sir Anthony Sherley's Journey ... as reported by two gentlemen who have followed him in the same the whole time of his travaile.* This work was apparently banned soon after it went on sale, probably because it lacked official permission. In 1601 it was followed by *A New and Large Discourse of the Travels of Sir Anthony Sherley ... by William Parry, Gentleman, who accompanied Sir Anthony in his Travells.* Then there was also a hand-written account by George Manwaring, another member of the group, but this was not printed until much later. All these, and perhaps other unknown sources, may have been used by Anthony Nixon who wrote a longer account of all three Sherley brothers, published in 1607.

Nixon was a prolific journalist (though this term did not exist at the time) who specialised in producing short 'newsbooks' on all kinds of current events, including the Gunpowder Plot of 1605, another pamphlet the same year titled *Oxford's triumph*, about James I's visit to Oxford, and, in 1609, *Newes from Sea, of two notorious Pyrats, Ward the Englishman and Danseker the Dutchman.* It is quite likely that Nixon's book on the Sherleys was promoted or encouraged by Thomas, the oldest brother, who returned to England a few months before it was published, after his painful years of imprisonment in Turkey.

Nixon did all he could to make heroes of all three of the brothers, arguing that their exploits were guided by motives of religion and honour. In his introduction to Anthony's story he wrote, 'his fame and renowne is known, and made glorious to the world by his honourable plots and imployments against the enemie of Christendome [i.e. Turkey]: which, according to the instructions I have received, I will briefly relate unto you.' A few pages later (Nixon's book is unpaginated) his description of this enemy was designed to suit existing public opinion: 'The Turks are beyond all measure a most insolent, superbous, and insulting people, ever prest to offer outrage to any Christian, if he be not well guarded with Janissaries. They sit at meat, as tailors upon their stalls, cross legged, and their meat served them upon the ground, passing the day for the most part in banqueting, and carousing.'

According to Nixon, the Persians were quite different. They, especially the Shah, looked very favourably on Christianity, so much so that he became godfather to Robert Sherley's son, and encouraged

Robert to set up an institution in which Persian children might be brought up as Christians.

Nixon gives brief accounts of Sir Anthony Sherley's journey to Persia, his reception by the Shah and his appointment as ambassador to the Christian monarchs of Europe. However, he skips Anthony's six-month stay in Moscow and his humiliating treatment by Czar Boris Godunov (perhaps as not befitting his hero), and takes the story straight from Persia to Prague. There is also a long description, which seems entirely invented, either by Nixon himself or perhaps one of his sources, of how Husein Beg, the Persian who had been Anthony Sherley's co-ambassador, returned to Persia, where Shah Abbas had his tongue and hands cut off because he had told lies about Anthony. Robert Sherley, who was said to be present, then suggested to the Shah that Beg also should also have his head cut off to save him from his misery. Nixon brings his narrative up to 1607, the year his book was published. He has Anthony travelling to Spain to meet the Spanish king (which was true), but fails to mention that the Queen had banned him from returning to England. Another section of the book deals with Thomas Sherley junior, and here there is enough convincing detail to suggest that Nixon got his information directly from Thomas himself. All in all, his account is a valuable source, but needs to be treated with extreme caution.

The same year that Nixon published his book, a play about the Sherley brothers, *The Travailes of the Three English Brothers*, was staged in one of the London theatres, probably the Red Bull. According to Samuel Chew, the Bull was 'a theatre which made a speciality of coarse, noisy, spectacular plays that appealed to rough folk,' though it seems doubtful whether *The Travailes* fell into this category. This was a corporate effort, written by John Day and two other playwrights. It is clear that its main source was Nixon, although the authors add (invent?) various other scenes and new characters. The play has been criticised for being shapeless and for disobeying the rules of dramatic art. One commentator describes it as 'a loose baggy monster with no natural shape,' and compares it unfavourably with Shakespeare's *Pericles* which was on at the *Globe* at the same time.[9] But one has to consider how difficult it must have been to construct a play about three brothers all having their adventures at different times and in different places. The solution favoured by Day was to give a leading role to a narrator, called variously Prologue, Fame or

Chorus, who explains to the spectators what is being enacted in front of them. At the start of the play Prologue begs the audience to help him by using their imaginations:

> First see a father parting with his sons,
> Then in a moment, on the full sails of thought
> We will divide them many hundred leagues,
> Our scene lies speechless, active but yet dumb
> Till your expressing thoughts give it a tongue …
> Imagine now the gentle breeze of heaven
> Hath on the liquid highway of the waves
> Conveyed him [Sir Anthony] many thousand leagues from us,
> Think you have seen him sail by many lands,
> And now at last arriv'd in Persia.

During the play there are conversations and disputes, but also scenes of battle and mock-battle, parades, banquets and brutal executions, in all of which the characters act in dumb show and the narrator helps us grasp what is happening.

Among the characters that are added to Nixon's narrative are Hallibeck, an evil Persian courtier who does his best to bring the downfall of Anthony and Robert, and also a Jew, Zariph, who has Anthony arrested for not paying back a loan. Another interesting character in the play is Will Kemp, who actually existed. This well-known comedian appears in a scene set in Venice as having just returned from a tour of Germany and Italy. He meets his old friend, Anthony Sherley: 'God save you, Master Kemp; welcome, Master Kemp, from dancing the morris over the Alps!' The two then proceed to discuss the state of the London stage.

It seems this meeting with Kemp did in fact take place, although in Rome, not Venice. Why Sherley and Kemp met, and whether they already knew each other, as the play suggests, is uncertain, but one possible explanation is that they might have been related, since the maiden name of Anne Sherley, Sir Anthony's mother, was Kemp(e). The literary historian Samuel Chew wonders whether Sir Anthony might already have mixed with London dramatists and actors before starting on his travels.[10] However, he certainly does not go as far as a certain nineteenth-century Yorkshire vicar, the Rev. Scott Surtees, who published a pamphlet suggesting that Sir Anthony was the author of Shakespeare's plays! (On both Will Kemp and Scott Surtees, see Appendix I).

One message of *The Travailes* seems to be that Persians are vastly superior to Turks, who are wicked infidels. True, Persians, like Turks, revere Mohammed, but their real religion is sun-worship. When a Persian courtier notices the Shah's interest in Christianity, he asks, perhaps in a reference to a pre-Islamic faith:

> Shall you whose empire for these thousand years
> Have given their adoration to the sun,
> The silver moon, and those her countless eyes,
> That like so many messengers wait on her,
> Forsake those lights perpetually abide?

Unlike Turks, Persians are said to look very favourably on Christianity as soon as they hear about it.

On the other hand, English gentlemen such as Anthony and Robert Sherley are definitely superior, even to Persians. For one thing, they introduced firearms into the country, which the Persians had never even heard of (not true; again, see Appendix I). And for another, these English are guided by a search for honour, which is why they do not kill those captured in battle, whereas the Persians always behead their captives, and stick their heads on spears. According to Casellas, this play makes clear that the Sherley brothers' voyages and adventures were to a great extent ruled by the pursuit of honour.[11] Yet this virtue was entirely new for the Persians: 'We never heard of honour until now,' says the Shah after Anthony explained to him what it meant.

The propagandist intention of *The Travailes* became difficult to sustain when the real nature of the three brothers' exploits became apparent for large sections of English society. As we have seen, there was sufficient evidence that, for the English government, Sir Anthony had already gone rogue, something that was finally demonstrated by his simultaneous services to various monarchs and his ignoring of English geo-political interests. By the time Day's play was put on stage, Sir Anthony had converted to Catholicism and was actually in the paid service of King Philip III of Spain (later he would also serve Philip IV). The latter information was briefly included in the epilogue of the play as a final comment by the Chorus (dressed as 'Fame'): 'Sir Anthony Sherley we have left in Spain/Knight of St Iago and Captain of th'Armado.' This was probably common knowledge at the time since it also appeared in Nixon's pamphlet.

The rumours of Sir Anthony's ambition to unite Europe against the Ottoman Empire, and of his reception by the Shah of Persia, especially when such rumours were spiced up in contemporary pamphlets and on the London stage, fitted in well with existing popular stereotypes regarding wicked and infidel Turks. But such sentiments hardly suited the Levant company merchants who traded with Turkey. Nor, sadly for Sir Anthony – and later for his younger brother, Robert – did they fit in with the policy of the Elizabethan government which shared in the profits of those merchants.

Chapter 13

Essex and honour

Sir John Falstaff muses to himself.
What is honour? A word.
What is in that word "honour"? What is that "honour"? Air.
A trim reckoning! Who hath it? He that died o' Wednesday.
Doth he feel it? No.
Doth he hear it? No.
'Tis insensible then? Yea, to the dead.
But will it not live with the living? No.
Why? Detraction will not suffer it.
Therefore I'll none of it. Honour is a mere scutcheon. And
  so ends my catechism.[1]

This chapter takes a look at the links between the career of Sir Anthony Sherley and that of Robert Devereux, 2nd Earl of Essex, also at the culture of honour in which they both participated, and the way it changed and became increasingly out of date even during their lifetimes. 'Honour' is a difficult concept for us today to grasp though we use the word itself often enough: 'the honourable gentleman for Lyme Regis,' 'honour among thieves,' 'I plead guilty, your honour.' When thinking about honour in the past one perhaps goes back to the great medieval estates with their hordes of dependents and tenants that were honour-bound to follow their lord into battle if called on to do so. The Northern rebellion of 1569 was the last of these feudal revolts that, if successful, could threaten the government of the day.[2] When the Earl of Westmorland, after some hesitation, decided to cast his lot with the rebels 'the house of Neville, in all its branches rose with him'.

The Earl of Essex, however, did not possess vast estates and armies of tenants that he could call on at will. Instead, he had to rely on his own aristocratic lineage and military career to create the role he sought for himself as a paragon of honour. As a young man he became the leader of an honour culture, which attracted members of leading gentry and noble families from a dozen counties who shared his values, and became his followers. One of these, from early days, was Anthony Sherley. Theirs was a creed of individual self-esteem and self assertiveness, in which one's honour was like a second skin that needed constant protection because it could be threatened or penetrated even more easily than the body itself. A passing remark that seemed to cast an aspersion on one's status, or perhaps on the morals of one's wife or daughter, could easily lead to a hand on the dagger, and worse. Yet, paradoxically, it was also a creed in which lineage played a major part. It mattered if you came from ancient stock. The honour of a gentleman had been transmitted to him through a line of ancestors, themselves all honourable men, and it was up to him never to disgrace them.

Anthony Sherley was born in 1565, the same year as Essex, his future hero and patron. Twenty years later both of them served in the Netherlands under Essex's step-father, the Earl of Leicester, and this is probably where they first met. Both took part in the famous encounter near Zutphen when a small group of English cavalry attacked a much larger Spanish force guarding the wagon train that was proceeding to the relief of the besieged town (see Chapter 2). Essex had already been appointed head of cavalry by Leicester, and he led repeated charges against the enemy. Sherley had temporarily left the company of which he was captain to join the group. This was the engagement in which Sir Philip Sidney, Leicester's nephew, and only a year or two older than Essex, though already famous for his gallantry and his poetry, received a mortal wound. Just before he died Sidney handed his sword to Essex, symbolically making him his heir as the champion of England against the hated Spanish, a role that Essex was to keep up during his future career. Not only that, but Essex cemented this connection by later marrying Sidney's widow.

Throughout his career Essex firmly believed that the king of Spain's ambitions posed a threat to the whole of Europe, and especially to England. No peace could hold with Spain because the Spanish word could not be trusted, and therefore the two countries must always be at war, either by sea or land. This was the conviction attacked by William Cecil, Lord Burghley, many years later when he named Essex a 'man of blood' for opposing the treaty of Vervins between France and Spain. Yet war was the setting in which a man of honour felt most at home. In war he could display his masculine virtues of courage, steadfastness, and loyalty to his comrades. Essex and his followers were contemptuous of the 'little men', the lawyers, bureaucrats and merchants who avoided danger and stayed at home while others fought.

When Leicester died in 1587 Essex was soon able to succeed him as Elizabeth's favourite young courtier, and through her influence he was able to acquire lands and offices, many of which could be passed on to his supporters. The downside of all this was that the Queen enjoyed his company so much that she was extremely reluctant to let him leave her and go off on the military and naval projects which his heart was set on. It was not until 1591 that she allowed him his first independent command. He was to cross the Channel to Dieppe with a force of 4,000. and join in the civil war that was raging between the newly crowned Henry IV and his Catholic opponents assisted by Spain. The campaign that followed did not achieve very much, and Essex found Elizabeth's flow of instructions to him both interfering and limiting. It became one of his constant themes, that a woman – even a queen – did not possess the necessary masculine qualities of determination and vigour, and therefore Elizabeth should never try to tell her commanders in the field what to do. However, this campaign gave Essex military experience, and it also allowed him to start what became a feature of all his future commands, which was to use his role as commander-in-chief to create new knights, who would then inevitably become members of his honour culture and look to him for future leadership.

Shortly before Essex's arrival in France, Anthony Sherley had also gained military experience. He took part in a three-month campaign under Lord Willoughby in which he was said to have fought bravely, and after a few months back in England he was given a more senior role in another campaign, this time in Brittany, where a Spanish force had landed at Saint-Nazaire. He was now in command of an entire regiment, one of three under the commander-in-chief, Sir John Norris. This campaign went on for some years and ended inconclusively, but before it ended Sherley had received a knighthood and found a wife, both of which must have greatly improved his status, especially among the followers of Essex. The marriage was with Essex's cousin, and the knighthood, although not granted by Essex himself, was from Henry IV of France, his close friend and ally. When the English authorities tried to cancel this award Sherley proclaimed that he would choose death rather than surrender the honour of knighthood (for the marriage and the knighthood see Chapter 2).

During 1596 and 1597 both Essex and Sherley took to the sea. In June 1596, Essex led an expedition to Cádiz, where a Spanish fleet was destroyed and the town captured. It was the most successful of all Essex's military and naval projects, and must have greatly increased his reputation. However, the Cádiz voyage was marred by arguments between Essex and Henry Howard, the joint leaders of the expedition. By now Essex had many enemies in the privy council, including Sir Walter Raleigh, and Robert Cecil, who was soon to succeed his father, Lord Burghley, as Elizabeth's Secretary of State. Essex believed that it was only by further military success that he could overcome this opposition, so in 1597 he organised and led another sea expedition against Spain. This was the Islands Voyage, the object of which was to sail to the Azores and there ambush the Spanish treasure fleet on its way to Spain from the Americas. However, misunderstandings and arguments among the leaders meant that the treasure fleet was missed. Anthony Sherley, just back from his unsuccessful privateering voyage, took part in this venture, and, in fact, was one of the principal officers of the expedition, and one of those whose vote nearly led to Raleigh's execution for allegedly disobeying Essex's commands.

After the failure of the Islands Voyage, Essex's position on Elizabeth's Privy Council became more and more problematic. His determination to take on Catholic Spain with the help of other like-minded nations was made impossible after both the Dutch and the French decided to make peace with Spain. At home, Elizabeth, too, appeared to support the majority of the council in rejecting Essex's aggressive foreign policy. Essex himself now suffered periods of depression in which he stayed away from council meetings, although he continued to search for ways of raising his own status by opposing Spanish power. He still saw himself as 'a man of great designs', and to facilitate his aims he had built up a network of agents throughout Europe who supplied him with the latest political and military information. One of the designs in which he involved himself was to dispatch a group of gentlemen adventurers to Ferrara where the duke had just died leaving the dukedom to his nephew, Cesare d'Este, who was opposed in the succession by Spain and the papacy. This was the group of which Essex had picked Anthony Sherley as leader. However, before they reached Ferrara news came that Cesare had surrendered his claim, so they made their way to Venice in search of other possible adventures.

Meanwhile, back at home another dilemma arose for Essex. In Ireland an English force had suffered a catastrophic defeat at the hands of a rebel Irish chieftain, the Earl of Tyrone, and it looked as if the whole of Ireland might fall to him unless something was done quickly. Who was to lead an English army to deal with Tyrone? To many, Essex seemed the obvious candidate and he certainly agreed. But he was in two minds, because he also believed that with himself out of the way in Ireland his enemies on the council would seize the chance to poison the Queen's mind against him. A crucial meeting took place in July 1598 between Elizabeth and her chief advisers, including Essex. When the Queen said something scornful about a candidate he had suggested for Ireland he turned his back on her, at which point she slapped him across the head, and instinctively he put his hand to his sword before being restrained by others. As he later explained to colleagues, to be struck by a woman was more than his honour could bear. After this meeting he withdrew himself from court and council for nearly two months until persuaded by his friends to return and accept the position of commander of the force that was being recruited to oppose Tyrone.

On 4 April 1599, Essex arrived in Dublin in charge of a large, though inexperienced, army. He decided to postpone an attack on Tyrone in Ulster until he had led his forces on a prolonged sweep into southern Ireland, partly to safeguard against a possible Spanish invasion. This project was successful, but it consumed time and resources, and left his troops exhausted and himself sick. He also received angry letters from the Queen asking why he was not following her specific instructions. Eventually he did advance to the north, but soon decided he lacked the necessary resources to take on Tyrone in the rapid campaign he had planned, so instead the two held a face-to-face parley on horseback. A truce was arranged, and Essex returned to Dublin. He realised Elizabeth would be furious, but believed that if he could only meet her in person he could justify his behaviour. So he left his army, and with only a few companions hurried back to London and the court. There ensued the famous – and fatal – encounter in which Essex, still muddy from his journey, rushed into Elizabeth's chamber one morning before she had done her hair or prepared herself for public viewing. That day was the last time Essex ever saw Elizabeth. He was confined to his house and subjected to hostile interrogations by members of the council.

Two months after Essex arrived in Dublin, Anthony Sherley left Venice on his dangerous journey to Persia, so it is unlikely that the earl would have had the time or inclination to write to his follower in foreign parts, even if he received a letter from him. Also, he might not have been particularly pleased by the new anti-Turkish policy that Sherley devised – most probably when he was travelling across Turkey to get to Persia. Although he continued to write to Essex it seems as if Sherley had cut himself off from his patron when he left Venice. It was not until he arrived in Archangel in May 1600, after having been held in Moscow for six months, that he heard about Essex's predicament. In his usual florid style he wrote to the earl concerning his continued devotion to him, 'If I be so happy as this letter may present itself before your Lordship's eyes, you shall see in it the constancy and fullness of my affection signed with that hand which no thing nor cause between heaven and earth shall ever alter.' He expressed his confidence that 'so rare and excellent virtue as your Lordship's can but receive a momentary eclipse.'[3] This letter was probably seized before it reached Essex, and the feelings Sherley expressed about his patron could hardly have improved his standing with Elizabeth's government.

After Essex had suffered months of confinement and questioning, during which the Queen dithered about his fate, he received a major blow in the autumn of 1600 when she refused to renew his lease of sweet wines from which he drew most of his income. He was ruined and his enemies had won. There was no alternative for him now, he felt, but to lead some kind of revolt, force a personal interview with Elizabeth, and persuade her to restore him to favour. Essex and his advisers decided to rely on his supposed popularity with the people of London. On 8 February 1601, Essex and about 300 supporters walked from Essex House on the Strand into the City, calling out to the spectators to join them in a march to Whitehall. But little enthusiasm was shown, and from then on everything went wrong. Essex was arrested and put on trial for treason. Less than three weeks later he was beheaded along with a handful of his colleagues.

Essex's trial revealed the fragility of the links between himself and his supporters. He started off by maintaining his role as the leader of a superior culture of honour, and by attacking his enemies as cowards of

Essex and honour

low birth. When Sir Robert Sidney was sent to Essex House to arrest him Essex told him, 'Judge you whether it can be grief to a man descended as I am, to be trodden underfoot by such base upstarts, men who keep aloof from danger, and dare not approach me.'[4] During his trial, however, he went through a volte-face. Under interrogation, the bonds of friendship and loyalty between him and leading members of his group started to dissolve when he and his closest colleagues gave evidence against one another. Essex accused both his sister, Penelope, and his chief secretary, Henry Cuffe, of having persuaded him to lead his march into the City. And when, on the scaffold, he came to deliver his final speech no mention was made of pride or honour, but instead Essex presented himself as an abject penitent who confessed his treason and humbly subjected himself to the religion and laws of his country. 'God,' he proclaimed, 'hath opened my eyes and made me see my sin, my offence, and so touched my heart as I hate it, both in myself and others.' Such was the sad end of what has been called the last honour revolt in England.[5]

Anthony Sherley was in Florence on his way to Rome when he heard the news. 'The Englishman was very much bound to the Count of Essex,' reported the Duke de Sessa, Spanish ambassador in Rome, 'and since the latter's imprisonment and death, he is completely without hope of ever again being admitted to the presence of the Queen.'[6] What, in fact, was now left for Anthony Sherley once the leadership and unity of his culture of honour had been broken in this humiliating fashion? Earlier, he had already cut himself off from his roots by travelling to Persia on his own initiative, and then designing a policy opposed to that of the English government.

His behaviour from now on suggests that for him all that remained of the old Essexian culture was an obsession with his own status together with a violent form of self-assertion when he feared this status was threatened in any way. There was, too, his claim to be a gentleman and a soldier rather than one of those whom Essex had labelled 'little men'. And, like his former patron, he was to have a continuing interest in pursuing grand designs rather than the short-term, profitable goals which he thought typical of merchants. In fact, he seemed to have retained a contempt for merchants and the moneyed class generally, to the extent that he never considered it dishonourable to move from one place to another, incurring debts as he went, with no intention of ever paying them back.

Isolated as he was, and cast aside by queen and country, Sherley needed to refashion himself rapidly in accordance with his new situation, using the skills he knew he possessed. He would be the agent of whatever master might employ him, without regard to nationality or religion. Sessa's report to King Philip III of Spain, mentioned above, shows this process was already underway: 'He is determined to serve your Majesty if your Majesty should so desire. He is a practical man and a good soldier on sea and on land. He has been to Persia and other places and he offers your Majesty important information.'[7] The path Sir Anthony had chosen would not be easy, especially for one having no country, few real friends, and above all no secure source of income, but he did his best, as the next chapter shows.

I conclude this chapter with a brief glance at why the Essexian culture of honour dissolved, and what was to succeed it. The Essex revolt failed, not so much because it was badly planned – though it was – but because of changes that had taken place in the social and political fabric of the nation during the sixteenth century. One change was the rapid growth in the numbers and power of Essex's 'base upstarts', the lawyers and officials who served the increasingly complex bureaucracy of the Tudor state. Accompanying and assisting this rise were numerous other factors, too complex to try and analyse here. They included: humanism and grammar schools, literacy and printed books, and the Protestant religion, with a bible in every household. Most important of all was the nationalisation of honour, which had now ceased to be exclusive to the upper classes or to men of war, but had become a virtue open to everyone. Honour now centred on the state, and was to be gained by all who served their queen and country. Under Elizabeth, Protestant England was seen to be a nation especially favoured by God (as the defeat of the Armada clearly proved), and therefore anyone who opposed the Queen or the law of the land was also going against divine will. Obedience had become a virtue to be cultivated above all others. Faced with this powerful and generally accepted ideology, it was little wonder that even an Essex could not hold out against it in the final moments of his life. Perhaps the only people who could flout such demands for ideological conformity were wealthy Catholic recusants in England with their priest holes, or those such as Anthony Sherley who had already severed the umbilical cord that linked him to his nation.

Chapter 14

Spying – a downward trajectory

We left Anthony Sherley in Ragusa, uncertain of his future, having abandoned his plan of travelling to Persia via Turkey. As explained above, he now no longer held any allegiance to his monarch or his country, and was looking for employment by a foreign prince – initially Philip III of Spain. By now he probably had no intention of ever returning to Persia, though he continued to correspond with Shah Abbas.

By now, too, he had renounced the religion of his boyhood and become a Roman Catholic. One cannot be sure when this conversion took place, and it may even have been three years earlier. Father Parsons, a Jesuit priest who knew Sir Anthony, wrote in a letter to another Jesuit that 'he denieth himself to have been a Protestant ever since his first being at Venice [in 1598] for that there he was reconciled [to Catholicism].'[1] Nor can we say whether this conversion was sincere, or merely convenient politically, as his one-time secretary, Giovanni Pagliarini, implied when, a few years later, he denounced his former employer as 'a man of no religion'.[2] There is a parallel here with Anthony's patron, Essex, who was accused at his trial not only of treason but of atheism, mainly on the grounds that many of his supporters were Catholic recusants, and that he supported toleration for Catholics.

Sherley now left Ragusa for Venice where he embarked on a new and highly precarious career. Venice was a cosmopolitan city, full of merchants as well as mercenaries and adventurers from every nation in Europe and beyond. For the next few years he seems to have worked as a free-lance intelligence agent and political adviser, without the slightest regard as to nation or religion. He contacted everyone he could think of, suggesting schemes for their nation's benefit or advising them of hostile plots. He offered to work for the French king, Henry IV, but without success. He wrote to James VI in Scotland offering his services, and to Emperor Rudolf in Prague. As mentioned in Chapter 11, he even had a conversation with the Spanish ambassador about how best to invade

England. On the other hand, he continued to send letters to Robert Cecil assuring him that he still offered his life to the Queen's service. 'No one,' he wrote, 'can be more an enemy of the King of Spain than myself.'[3] And he continued writing to Shah Abbas.

But Cecil, for one, no longer trusted Sir Anthony – if he ever had. Cecil ran a wide network of agents supplying him with information, and now he set one of his best 'intelligencers', Thomas Wilson, to watch over Sherley, who retaliated by spying on him, so effectively that Wilson wrote to Cecil, 'I am forced at this present to change my lodging, and live very retired and make it be given out that I am gone out of town, only to shun his impudent company, which intrudes himself every day by force, only to spy on me, whether I know of his practices.'[4]

Another of Cecil's agents in Venice, Aurelian Townsend, a young gentleman who later became a well-known poet, was instructed to befriend Sherley and find out what he could. But Townsend was not an efficient spy and he fell victim to Shelley's charm. 'I have several times informed you,' he wrote to Cecil, 'of the loss I have sustained by lending two hundred scudi to Sir Anthony Sherley ... but if you knew how cunningly he laid the net in which finally I was entangled, you would not wonder that a young man like me was not strong enough to resist the affection, the consideration, and the promises of Sir Anthony.'[5]

By about 1602 Sir Anthony was probably receiving payments from both the Spanish and the Scottish monarchs, though how regular and how much these payments were we do not know. He also tried other ways of earning a living. At one point he went into partnership with an alchemist, and the two of them persuaded various friends to invest in 'a secret method for the refinement of silver-containing metals without the use of quicksilver.'[6]

The income of a self-employed intelligencer was insecure, and so, apparently, was his life. In August 1602 Anthony reported to various correspondents that an assassin in the pay of Turkey had fired an arquebus through a window and narrowly missed him Thomas Wilson, however, produced for Cecil another version of the incident: 'He being one time in my chamber there was shot into the window by a little boy an earthen bullet, out of a wooden crossbow such as boys use here, which hitting upon the wall and the noise making us look about, we found in the wall the print of a bullet [and] looking well about, we found the broken earthen bullet, and afterwards I understood how it was shot.'[7]

At another time, when walking one summer evening near a canal, Sir Anthony and two friends were set upon by ruffians. One of them was badly wounded and Anthony himself was thrown, or jumped to save himself, into the canal. He was almost drowned when his cloak became entangled round his head, but was able to keep afloat until help arrived. Anthony himself reported to his correspondents that this murderous attack also was organised by Turkey. Predictably, Wilson came up with a different explanation: 'I have heard since it was by the procurement of a fellow which had let him have for 40 or 50 ducats in wine, and finding no means to get his money, vowed to have his blood and the rest which had nourished their blood with his wine: and so indeed they will do here to such where they can get no other remedy.'[8]

Anthony also believed that Wilson himself planned to kill him, which was not far from the truth. In one letter to Cecil Wilson said: 'Whereas I wrote another time that, to prevent his dangerous devices my courage would serve to do anything you should command me ... my meaning was not to get him killed here, but if you should like of getting him into an *England* ship and send him home, or any such other means whereby the truth of all matters might be made apparent, in such case my courage would serve me to venture my life to apprehend him by force.' He could, he said, easily persuade the Venetian authorities to overlook this kidnapping, 'and to that purpose I made acquainted withal one of the greatest men of this State, that the State might not apprehend the matter as an injury to offer such violence in their dominion.'[9] Such was the life of an intelligencer.

Meanwhile, the Venetian authorities were becoming increasingly exasperated with Sir Anthony's activities, and in the spring of 1603 they arrested him on the grounds that he had sent armed men to force a newly arrived Persian merchant to sell him a consignment of silk. About this time, too, his standing in Venice was not improved by the discovery that he was the brother of that Sir Thomas Sherley, whose piracy in the Mediterranean had included attacks on Venetian ships. A lengthy investigation ensued, the details of which have been uncovered by D. W. Davies in the Venetian state archives. They show how adept Sir Anthony was, when under interrogation, at producing answers that sounded convincing. The following extract is about his relations with his brother Thomas's wife, Frances, who had recently died:

> Question: "Did you know about [Sir Thomas's] departure from England?"
> Answer: "No, most illustrious sir, for seven years I have heard nothing."
> Question: "When did you receive your last letter from him?"
> Answer: "I have known nothing about him for seven years. My brother married against my wishes. His wife has persecuted me. I have often fought duels with her brother, Thomas Vavasour, and both of us have been injured in the fighting. I heard recently that a relative of this woman, named Charles, has arrived in Venice. He intends to harm me in order that the property may go to the children of that woman and not to me [clearly the Vavasour family were expecting Sir Thomas's imminent death in a Turkish prison]. These matters are the reason for my leaving England; my brother was supported by Secretary Cecil and I by the Earl of Essex.'[10]

Did the Venetian commissioners believe Sir Anthony's story? Possibly. Do we today believe it? Almost certainly not.

James I, who had just succeeded to the throne, and who was inclined to favour the Sherleys, who had been in touch with him since before he became King of England, now wrote to the Doge and Council of Venice requesting that, unless Sir Anthony had actually conspired against the state of Venice, he should be considered for release. We are told, too, that Sir Anthony was now in ill health, suffering from kidney disease.[11] For one, or both of these reasons, in May 1603 Sir Anthony found himself released from prison, to continue his activities as a freelance agent. He started spying again, this time for the Emperor Rudolf in Prague, furnishing him with reports on the Turkish forces, which he himself received from a contact in Constantinople. At this time Rudolf's forces were fighting the Turks in Hungary, so information about Turkey's military strengths and weaknesses was particularly welcome. But to the Venetians this was intolerable, because it jeopardized their policy of avoiding trouble with the Ottomans, a cornerstone of their diplomacy.

On 1 December 1604, Sherley was summoned to appear before the council and given four days to leave the city, never to return under pain of death. This time James I did not intervene, and Sir Anthony went to Ferrara, from where he continued his correspondence with potential patrons.

Early in 1605 prospects suddenly improved for him when he was summoned to Prague, initially to assist in negotiations between the emperor and a newly arrived Persian diplomat.. He spent several weeks in Prague, and by the time he left his status had risen again. Now he was no longer a spy living off his wits, but once again a real ambassador. Rudolf sent him to Morocco as the joint representative of himself, Philip III of Spain and James I of England. He was to receive an income from the first two, and James wrote to English merchants in Morocco requesting them to supply him with any necessities and with credit if required. There were also some Austrian horse breeders who gave him funds to buy Arab horses for them (which he never did). All in all, Anthony had never been so well-funded since Essex gave him £8,000 for the Ferrara project.

Morocco at this time was no longer the settled and peaceful state that it had been some years earlier when English merchants made large profits by trading in sugar and other commodities. The King, El Mansour, who had once sent his ambassador to London, had died of the plague, and his three sons were engaged in fighting an anarchic civil war with each other to decide the succession. Sir Anthony was instructed to meet with one of these sons, Moulay Abu Fares, who had based himself in the capital, Marrakesh, where he called himself king of Morocco. The idea was to make friends with him, offer him help in his struggles against his two brothers, and then persuade him to make war against the Ottoman Turks who controlled ports along the Moroccan coast. The ultimate purpose of this project was to make the Turks divert their attention to North Africa and so take some of the pressure off Hungary where they were still fighting Rudolf's forces.

Sir Anthony set off for Morocco in July 1605 with a group of thirteen that included various interpreters, and also a young friend of his whom he had met in Venice, Sir Edwin Rich. The journey to Morocco was awkward and dangerous owing to Mediterranean storms which damaged the ship they were in, so that it had to be abandoned at Alicante while they travelled overland to Cádiz, and from there hired another ship to get to the port of Safi on the Atlantic coast of Morocco. At Safi they had to wait several weeks until Abu Fares sent 500 soldiers to escort them to Marrakesh. There Sir Anthony was treated with all the honour he felt he deserved as ambassador, and soon found it easy to discuss his mission with the self-styled King. After a magnificent entry into the city he was assigned a large house near the El Badi Palace, which had been built by El Mansour. This palace, modelled on the Alhambra in Granada, had 360 richly decorated rooms, as well as a vast entrance hall. Apparently, only the King himself was allowed to ride on horseback through this hall, and even his relations had to leave their horses at the door. However, on his first visit Sir Anthony decided not to observe this convention. A contemporary pamphlet takes up the story:

> Reasonably attended, he rode to court, not lighting from his horse where the King's sons usually do, but rode through the *Mushward*, which is the King's great hall, which none but the King himself doth. Being come into the King's presence, his letters of credit were received with great show of kindness, and himself entertained with all gracious respect … Some five days after, Sir Anthony Sherley coming to audience, and thinking to have ridden in as he did before, a chain was hung across the entrance of the *Mushward*, which he perceiving only done to hinder his passage, would not alight from his horse, but returned back very discontented … The blame was laid upon the King's porter, offering Sir Anthony the porter's head if he would have it; so spending an hour to pacify his choler, and bring him back, the porter before his face was sore beaten and imprisoned, neither ever after was he hindered of riding through the *Mushward*.[12]

Sir Anthony stayed five months in Marrakesh, during which time he got to know Abu Fares well, though his actual mission was unsuccessful. However, typically of him whenever he had money to spend, he made himself into a well-known and popular figure through his extravagant hospitality to everyone he came across. For example, he gave a new turban to each of the 500 soldiers whom Abu Fares had sent to escort him to Marrakesh. As the pamphlet already quoted explains: 'Whilst he was amongst them, he behaved himself very well towards those of better sort, winning credit with them, and gaining the love of the poorer sort exceedingly by his largess. For if a Moor or slave gave him but a dish of dates, he should receive a reward as from an Emperor, and howsoever some may hold this a vice, counting him a lavisher, yet by this means he came to the knowledge of that which otherwise he never should have attained unto.'[13]

There were perhaps two reasons for the failure of Sir Anthony's mission. One concerned the nature of Abu Fares. 'The King,' wrote Sherley to Emperor Rudolf, 'is of a pusillanimous, cowardly, fearful disposition and not at all warlike.'[14] Actually, he lived in daily fear of being attacked from Fez by his brother, Moulay ech-Cheik. Therefore, he certainly had no intention of making war on a new enemy, and in fact hoped to enlist the Turks as allies against his two brothers. The other reason concerned Emperor Rudolf who had sent Sir Anthony to Morocco in the first place. Throughout his reign Rudolf had suffered from mental instability, and in 1605 he was forced by other family members to cede control of Hungarian affairs to his younger brother, Matthias, who the following year made peace with the Turks and withdrew his forces from Hungary. Consequently, Sir Anthony's mission – to stir up war between Morocco and Turkey – had become entirely redundant.

In August 1606, Sir Anthony left Safi for Lisbon. He had not only spent all his money, but, in his typical style, had accumulated debts from various merchants. With him were two Portuguese noblemen who had been held prisoner in Morocco for many years and whom he managed to ransom on the understanding they would repay him when they reached Portugal. But once in Lisbon the two broke their contract. 'These gentlemen signed with me', Sir Anthony wrote to Robert Cecil, 'and now I am come here they do not only deny to pay, but persecute me as much as they dare and can, with all the vile usage that can be devised.'[15] We don't know exactly what that persecution entailed, but in Anthony Nixon's booklet about the three Sherley brothers published in 1607, as well as the play about them that was staged in London the same year, it is alleged that one of the freed prisoners tried (unsuccessfully) to poison their benefactor rather than paying him what they owed.

Sir Anthony now made his way to Madrid to explain to Philip III the failure of his Moroccan mission, as well as how he had been mistreated in Lisbon. In spite of being bankrupt he managed a triumphal entry into Madrid, 'accompanied by a suite of thirty, splendidly dressed'.[16] However, his lack of money meant that for the next few weeks he had to give up the lavish lifestyle he much preferred. The Venetian ambassador reported that 'his debts compel him to live very quietly in his house and greatly diminish the repute he originally acquired by his splendour of living.'[17] Nevertheless, he was treated with respect by the King and his ministers, and spent the time proposing various schemes which might benefit Spain (and himself). One scheme that was actually taken up by Philip III and his ministers was to make Sherley 'Captain General of the Mediterranean Sea', with power to provide a fleet of ships to protect Naples and Sicily from the raids of Turks and pirates. His commission stated: 'That for as much as the King is resolved to disturb the trade of the Hollanders in the Levant Seas, & withal to infest the common enemies of Christendom the Turks & Moors, he hath to that end made choice of Don Anthonio Sherley, as a man experienced in marine services &c. to be General of all his Comands; all his Viceroys, & all his Ministers of Justice to acknowledge him, to give him free entry into all his Majesties Towns & Ports, to aid him in levying of men, victualing of ships &c.'[18]

In view of his previous naval experiences, which included the unsuccessful privateering expedition of 1596 and his participation in Essex's equally unsuccessful 'Islands Voyage' the following year (both against Spain), it does seem rather surprising he was chosen for this prestigious naval role. It is true that some of the Spanish ministers felt Sherley was an extravagant and restless character who could not be relied on to do what he was proposing, but the danger from pirates was such that it was finally agreed to allow him to proceed with his suggested plan, which was to allow him to import cloth into Spain duty free, sell it, and spend the profits on acquiring ten ships and their crews, which could then be used to protect Naples and Sicily from pirates. He hoped to recruit English sailors to man these ships, particularly since many ex-privateers were available as, after 1604, they were no longer allowed to prey on Spanish ships because James I had signed peace with Spain. At one point he even tried to enlist help from two notorious pirates, Ward and Dauncer[19], but this proved unsuccessful.

For the next two years Sir Anthony proceeded slowly with his project, buying ships and searching for suitable crews. He had enemies who resented his new appointment, not only Turks and Venetians but also many English, including Sir Charles Cornwallis, the English ambassador in Madrid, whose frequent sarcastic letters to Cecil about him are in the state papers. Another enemy was his former secretary, Pagliarini, who had quarrelled with his employer and returned to Venice where they had first met. As Sir Anthony wrote to his sister, Anne (who had married Sir John Tracy of Toddington, Gloucestershire), excusing himself for not having written to her earlier: 'You will say I should have written – it is true – but there are such intercepting of my papers that before God I dare commit nothing to paper, and now less than ever; that villain Pagliarrino who received so great favour from you at Toddington, being run from me with all my papers, and disclosed to my good friend the Venetian much of the King of Spain's secret and own business.'[20]

Sir Anthony travelled extensively at this time. In 1607 he went to Naples, then to Prague to report to the emperor about the failure of the Moroccan project. Rudolf presumably did not hold this failure against him, as he ennobled him, conferring on him the title of Count Palatine. Then it was back to Madrid, and finally, in 1609, to Palermo, to meet the Spanish viceroy of Sicily, the Duke of Escalonia, who was nominally his superior but who had been ordered by the King to assist him by every means possible. Inevitably, there was soon friction, and then outright hostility, between these two proud noblemen (one of them of the old Spanish nobility, the other so recently ennobled). To find the crews and the ships seemed to take forever, and both Sherley and Escalonia wrote to Madrid complaining bitterly about what each was doing, or not doing. So did Pagliarini from Venice: 'This affair is all smoke and vanity ... He [Sherley] seeks to cover up the fact that he has not armed and furnished a fleet as he promised your Catholic Majesty. Don Antonio couldn't furnish and arm a rowboat ... He is a man who affects an air of mystery in everything.'[21]

But finally the ships were ready at Syracuse, with Italian and Spanish soldiers prepared to board them. It was a dangerous time because, apart from this little squadron, Sicily lacked any naval protection whatever, and it was rumoured that pirates were preparing raids. The problem was that all shipping in Naples and Sicily had been ordered to Spain to assist in the expulsion of Spanish Moriscoes to Africa. These were people of Moslem origin who had originally converted to Christianity, but who were now being blamed for the decline of the Spanish economy. Sherley was ordered by both the King and Escalonia not to delay any longer, but to set sail in search of pirates. He was specifically ordered to stick to naval engagements, and not to try and invade Turkish territory.

However, this is precisely what he did, taking on Turkish forces on the islands of Sciatos and Lesbos, with consequent losses. On this trip he also experienced storms, and some of his ships were badly damaged. To make things worse he also seized a Venetian ship, selling its cargo in Palermo, whereby the Venetians complained vigorously to Spain. When the Spanish authorities heard about all this they decided that Sir Anthony's remaining vessels should remain in port and that he himself be removed from command. This was the end of his last naval venture, and the end of his employment by the Spanish state in any capacity. Sir Anthony returned to Spain in January 1611, to be awarded a small annual pension and requested to retire to Granada, a long way from the Spanish court.

A month after arriving in Granada he heard that his brother Robert had just arrived in Madrid as ambassador for Shah Abbas, and had been treated well by the authorities, receiving generous funding and a house in the capital. Anthony immediately decided to return to Madrid to meet him, and there then took place an episode which reflects no credit at all on the elder brother. This I will postpone until Chapter 17.

Chapter 15

Abbas the Great

Abbas I was a monarch worthy to be ranked with other great contemporary rulers such as Elizabeth I of England, the Moghul Emperor Akbar and Suleyman the Magnificent. He died in January 1629, having reigned for thirty years longer after he dispatched Anthony Sherley to Europe as his ambassador. During this time he achieved enough for posterity to label him 'Abbas the Great', and this chapter covers a few of the achievements that justify this title.

Although he had comprehensively defeated the Uzbeks in the east in 1598, it was not until 1605 that Abbas felt strong enough to attack the Ottomans in the west, but when he did success was rapid. He proceeded in successive campaigns to expel the last Turkish soldier from Persian territory as defined by the treaty made by Shah Tamasp in 1555; peace was finally signed with the Ottomans in 1618. Abbas believed in a hands-on style of military command, and this, coupled with his success, undoubtedly increased his status among the people, allowing him to complete his reforms of the Persian state. As he once told the Italian traveller, Pietro Della Valle, in the course of criticising Philip II of Spain and his withdrawn style of leadership: 'An emperor must himself be a soldier and personally lead troops onto the battle-field. A ruler cannot leave the destiny of his country in the hands of his ministers and army chiefs. Such a king is bound for misfortune.'[1]

In spite of this military success, it is also true that Persian forces at this time had significant weaknesses. For a start, the country had no navy, nor even a merchant fleet, which is why, when Abbas wanted to capture the island of Hormuz – at the entrance to the Persian Gulf – from the Portuguese, he had to persuade the English East India Company to help him (see below). Secondly, Persian armies had been transformed to a lesser extent by the introduction of modern weaponry, especially large guns, than the armies of other Eastern empires. As Michael Axworthy explains, 'Their cavalry usually outclassed that of their enemies, but

Persians did not take to heavy cannon and the greater technical demands of siege warfare as the Ottomans and Moghuls did. The great distances, lack of navigable rivers, rugged terrain and poor roads of the Iranian plateau did not favour the transport of heavy cannon. Most Iranian cities were either unwalled or were protected by crumbling walls centuries old – at a time when huge, sophisticated and highly expensive fortifications were being constructed in Europe and elsewhere to deal with the challenge of heavy cannon. Persia's military revolution was left incomplete.'[2.] Such weaknesses were to be felt, if not so much by Abbas, as by his successors.

From the moment he became leader, Abbas knew he had to impose his authority on the Qizilbash tribes and their amirs, or remain their tool. But the Qizilbash were still the backbone of the Safavid forces; if he weakened them, he undermined the state. His solution was to greatly expand the standing army of *ghulams* which his predecessor, Shah Tahmasp, had started. These were Georgian, Armenian, and Circassian Christians who were taken prisoner in large numbers during the Safavid campaigns in the Caucasus, converted to Islam, trained for military service, and then settled in the Persian heartland. For instance, it is reckoned that around 330,000 of these *ghulams* and their families had been captured during Abbas's Georgian campaign of 1614-15. Their loyalty was to the Shah, not to a tribal leader, and they were therefore a valuable support to him in his disputes with the Qizilbash.

To create this new standing army instead of relying on the Qizilbach tribes whenever there was a war was expensive. To deal with this, plus all the other charges of court and administration, Abbas undertook various reforms to improve the economy, and therefore increase revenue. For instance, he took many provinces away from their Qizilbash amirs and put them directly under government control, which greatly increased the proportion of taxation which actually ended up in his treasury. He also spent a lot of energy developing better trade conditions for both local and foreign merchants. He improved the roads, built new ones, and set up a network of *caravanserais* – lodging houses where merchants and their servants and animals could stay the night for free – on main routes and in cities. Security was also greatly enhanced by the rule that any traveller who had goods stolen must be reimbursed by the local governor. The country soon became notable for the safety of its roads.

Unusually for a monarch, whether eastern or western, Abbas took a close interest in everything connected with trade, and in fact engaged in trade himself. Pietro Della Valle called him 'the greatest merchant in his Kingdom'. Persia's main export was raw silk, which was just as important to the country as oil is today. Royal agents took over a large part of the silk industry, which Abbas did everything he could to encourage. For instance, he forcibly resettled hundreds of families from the Caucasus region to the province of Mazandaran, south of the Caspian Sea, where he encouraged them to produce silk, planting large numbers of mulberry trees for the silk worms to feed on. Europe was the main market for Persian silk, and it was Christian merchants from Armenia who had previously dominated the trade, transporting the bales of raw silk to Aleppo, where it was bought by European merchants and carried across the Mediterranean. Many of these Armenians saw their homes destroyed in the course of the wars between Persia and Turkey, owing to the Shah's scorched earth policy of denying supplies to advancing Ottoman armies. This applied to the city of Julfa (now in Azerbaijan) where, in 1604, the entire population, mainly Armenians, was expelled, and every house pulled down. The town crier announced the following expulsion order: 'The great King, Shah Abbas, orders you to leave and move to the land of the Persians. If you move within three days, we shall treat you leniently. Those who are found here after three days will be killed and their families and their belongings will become captives. If anyone flees or hides, his property shall be given to the person who points him out and his head will be sent to the Shah.'[3]

Abbas created a new suburb of Isfahan called New Julfa where homeless Armenians, especially silk merchants, were encouraged to settle and given special privileges. These merchants were particularly important to the Shah because their silk was sold in exchange for silver, a commodity Persia traditionally lacked. It was by taxing them that Abbas acquired the silver he needed to pay his armies and meet his ambitious building expenses. The Persian silk industry, now divided between the Armenians and the Shah's own agents, became increasingly successful during Abbas's reign.

After his victory over the Uzbeks in 1598, Abbas moved his capital from Qazvīn to Isfahan, which he transformed into one of the most beautiful cities in the world. He created the Royal Square, a vast urban space surrounded by newly built palaces and mosques, and next to it, through an ornate gateway, the large domed hall of the Grand Market, where visitors from all over the world flocked to buy the luxury goods created by Persian craftsmen. Impressive, too, was the Chahar Bagh, a fifty-yard wide avenue that ran for three miles from one of the city gates to the foothills of the mountains in the south. It crossed the Zayandeh (the river that supplied Isfahan with its water) by a long, elegant bridge named after its creator, the Shah's ghulam general, Allaverdi Khan. This new avenue was surrounded by parks and gardens, and just to its west was the suburb of New Julfa with its Christian churches and its mansions belonging to wealthy Armenian merchants.

During the reign of Abbas, Isfahan prospered and its population went up from 50,000 to about 200,000, including many foreigners. The Shah's motives for all his investment in the city were, of course, political and economic as much as aesthetic. As one historian explains, 'Isfahan was much more than simply the beautiful city that Iranians today still refer to as *nisf-a jahan*, or "half the world". The king's mosque, the Ali Qapu gateway, the Shaykh Luftallah Mosque, the grand bazaar, and the other building projects that Shah Abbas sponsored not only reveal the aesthetics of architecture and artistic creativity fostered in the Safavid period, but they also reflect notions of Safavid Kingship and authority, the relationship between religion and the state, and the position of commerce and trade in Iran.'[4] In other words, the scope and layout of the new Isfahan was designed to show its status as the capital of a powerful Islamic empire, as well as to boost Abbas's authority. And his passion for building was demonstrated not only in Isfahan but also by the raising of numerous utilitarian structures all over the country: caravanserais, cisterns, bathhouses, bridges, roads, hospitals, schools, and other public works – not to mention the large sums he invested in the Shia pilgrimage sites at Ardabil and Mashad.

Abbas also developed a system of workshops which produced a range of goods for the domestic market and for export, including textiles, carpets and ceramics. These royal workshops were concentrated mainly in Isfahan. The craftsmen working in them were well paid, and there was fierce competition to become members. Many of the products went in gifts to local grandees or to other monarchs such as Akbar (1556-1605), the Moghul ruler of India. To take one example of an initiative shown by Abbas in this craft area, he noticed the high demand throughout Europe for Chinese blue-and-white porcelain vases and dishes, so he imported

300 Chinese craftsmen who could instruct Persians in the techniques of porcelain manufacture. This was so successful that it became hard for buyers to distinguish Chinese porcelain from Persian copies.

The most prestigious of these workshops was the Royal Library, in which Abbas was particularly interested. This held a magnificent collection of manuscripts and books, and a large team of painters, bookbinders and calligraphers worked there. Abbas also encouraged his courtiers and nobles to follow his example and become patrons of the arts, with their own specialist architects and artists. He would sometimes demand that an artist employed by someone else work for him instead. Ali Reza was a talented young calligrapher employed by the Qizilbash amir, Farhad Khan, when Abbas invited him instead to join the Royal Library as head calligrapher. Ali Reza was later chosen to inscribe texts on the walls of the two famous mosques in Isfahan's Royal Square. He became the Shah's close friend, and it is said that when he was working at night Abbas would sometimes join him and hold a candle while he wrote. But inevitably, among the factions in the Library there was rivalry and jealousy, and one night another leading calligrapher, Mir Imam, was murdered by ruffians, most likely on orders from the Shah, on request from his favourite, Ali Reza.[5]

One remarkable feature of Persian culture in the time of the Safavids was the way it spread beyond the borders of Persia. For instance, numbers of artists, poets and others emigrated to the court of the Moghul emperors in India, where they found lucrative employment. Many were fleeing from the increasingly narrow orthodoxy of the Shia mullahs in Persia, as compared with the more tolerant religious policy of Akbar. Others found that their poetry was more appreciated at the Moghul court than at home, especially as Persian was the language of this court. Abbas himself seemed less interested in poetry than in the more practical arts – perhaps because poetry had less obvious commercial benefits.

One of Shah Abbas's greatest achievements was to set up channels of communication between Persia and the West. His capital, Isfahan, became frequented by European ambassadors, by merchants seeing trading privileges, by Catholic friars from Italy wanting permission to open convents and carry on missionary activity, and, of course, by gentlemen adventurers such as the Sherley brothers, and travellers such as Pietro della Valle, who left valuable accounts of Safavid Iran. Abbas was always keen on meeting visitors from Europe, and questioning them about the countries they came from. With his particular interest in the economy, he wanted, whenever possible, to encourage trade with the West.

As we know, the Shah's other main ambition, for which he exchanged ambassadors and wrote numerous letters to Western princes, was to persuade European powers to cooperate with him in war against the Ottomans. It was for this purpose, for instance, that he employed Anthony Sherley, and later his younger brother, Robert (see the next chapter), but here he was never successful, perhaps because communication between Persia and Europe was too difficult, but also because European nations were often preoccupied with their own quarrels. However, what he did do was to open up Persia to the West, so that educated Europeans could buy Persian goods, read about Persia, and even visit the country. It is important to realise, too, that this was perhaps the last time that nations like Persia conducted diplomatic and commercial relations with the West on a basis of equality. The Safavid empire, along with the Ottoman and Moghul empires, can be seen as the final flowering of early modern Islamic civilisation before the technological superiority of the West ushered in the age of western imperialism and the domination of much of the Islamic world.[6]

Before leaving Persia there is just enough time to mention three triumphs gained by Abbas during his final years. Since the start of the sixteenth century the Portuguese had controlled trade in the Indian Ocean and the Red Sea from their base, the island of Hormuz at the mouth of the Persian gulf. Towards the end of his reign, Abbas became increasingly resentful of Portuguese wealth and power, especially after his royal agents had come to dominate the Persian silk industry. He disliked the fact that most of the silk exported from Persia had to pass through Hormuz, and then through Ottoman territory on its way to Europe, paying heavy duties to potential, or actual, enemies as it went. When the British East India Company, founded in 1600, showed interest in the silk trade, Abbas saw his opportunity to capture Hormuz, and alter the flow of silk away from Turkey to the new sea route via the Cape of Good Hope. The EIC owned the warships without which any attack on this well-guarded island was impossible, so Abbas made a deal with them, offering favourable trade terms in return for help against the Portuguese.

In February 1622, a large Persian force landed on Hormuz while EIC ships bombarded the fortified citadel and the Portuguese ships sheltering under it. Within a few weeks the siege was over and the Portuguese surrendered. Having captured the island, Abbas transferred its trade to Gombroon, a port on the mainland which was easier to defend, and which was renamed Bandar Abbas (the port of Abbas). The English, soon to be joined by their rivals, the Dutch East India Company (VOC), took over a large share of Persian silk for export to Europe, although Armenian merchants from New Julfa continued to handle their part of the trade through Ottoman centres such as Aleppo.

Two other successes that Abbas gained before he died were the taking of Baghdad to the west, and of Kandahar on Persia's eastern frontier. Baghdad had been under Ottoman rule since the reign of Tahmasp, but the opportunity to reclaim it arose when the Ottoman Empire was thrown into chaos after the assassination of its Sultan in 1620. The recapture of Baghdad and its region was important to the Persians since it included the Shi'ite shrines of Karbala and Najaf. However, this area, which is part of central Iraq today, proved difficult for the Safavids to retain permanently, being separated from the rest of Persia by the Zagros mountains, and Baghdad and the shrines were back under Turkish control within ten years after the death of Abbas.

As mentioned above, Abbas on the whole maintained cordial relations with the Moghuls in India. However, they did disagree over who owned the city of Kandahar (in present-day Afghanistan). This city had been taken by Akbar in 1594, at a time when Abbas was too weak to resist. It was an important trading centre on the route between Persia and the East, and Abbas was determined to retrieve it. In 1622 he felt strong enough to move against Akbar's son and successor, Jahangir. He led his army to Kandahar, which surrendered after a five week siege, remaining in Persian hands until the early eighteenth century.

Abbas ceased to follow the traditional Safavid practice of appointing the sons of the Shah to provincial governorships, with each prince in the care of a Qizilbash amir who acted as his guardian and was responsible for his education. Instead, he confined his sons to the royal harem, where they were brought up by the women of the King's household and by eunuchs. This system was open to various objections: it gave rise to harem intrigues, which were often more serious than the occasional revolt of a provincial governor, and it denied the royal princes the opportunity of gaining experience of government, with the result that, when called to the throne, they proved incompetent. As his obsessive fear of assassination increased towards the end of his life, Abbas resorted to an even crueller practice than mere confinement in the royal harem. He either put to death or blinded any member of his family who aroused his suspicion; in this way one of his sons was executed and two blinded. Consequently, when he died in 1629 there was only a grandson, Prince Sam, to succeed him, and this grandson ruled as Shah Safi I (1629-42).

To conclude, Abbas did possess qualities which entitle him to be styled 'the Great'. He was a pragmatist in all things, whether they related to religion, politics, or commerce, to civilian or military matters. Unlike his grandfather, Shah Ṭahmasp, he never allowed religious bigotry to interfere with trade. He was a brilliant strategist and field commander whose chief characteristic was prudence. Though personally a brave man, he would never have led his cavalry in a wild charge against the Ottoman guns as did his great-grandfather, Ismail I, in the disastrous defeat at Calderan back in 1514. If Abbas could achieve his ends by diplomacy rather than war, he preferred to do so, and was prepared to wait years to achieve his objectives, as he did with Hormuz, Baghdad and Kandahar.

Due to its firm foundations, provided largely by Abbas, the Safavid dynasty lasted for another century, but under its last two shahs serious problems arose, including neglect of the army and irreconcilable divisions between rival political factions. In 1722 twenty thousand Afghan horsemen laid siege to Isfahan and starved the city into surrender. Chaos and further war ensued, until a new dynasty, the Quajars, took over.

Chapter 16

Robert Sherley

We now come to the adventures of Robert, youngest of the three Sherley brothers and sixteen years younger than Anthony. When Anthony left Persia in 1599 as ambassador for Shah Abbas, Roger was about eighteen, although he had already spent several years in Florence before being invited to come to Venice to join Anthony on his Persian expedition. Now, he was to remain in Persia together with a few other Englishmen from the original group, including his friend, Captain Thomas Powell, a specialist in gunnery Keeping Robert in Persia was perhaps seen by Abbas as a guarantee that Anthony would return on the completion of his mission. So far as we know, Robert never wrote an account of his adventures, as did Anthony and even Thomas, but something can be gleaned from the letters he wrote and received.

To start with, his character. During his years in Persia he seems to have made himself popular by his politeness to all and his sensitivity to native customs. This, at least, was the verdict of a Carmelite monk who had known him in Isfahan: 'In Persia he had gained the goodwill of the King and of the nobles, by whom he is liked because he renders service to all and sundry, and gives trouble to nobody; besides which he conformed to their habits and customs in things that were not contrary to our religion.'[1] As this account implies, when in Persia Robert did his best to behave like a Persian. He always dressed like a Persian nobleman, including the turban, and he went on doing so when he left the country as the Shah's ambassador. He also married a Turkish lady, as will be discussed in a moment. Furthermore, as the years passed he seems to have mastered the language. In one of his letters to Anthony, written in 1606, he enclosed a document in Persian, and adds in the letter 'becaus haply in thos places you live in, you shal fynde fewe, or none at al to translat them unto you, I will breefly declare unto you the circomstance of it.'[2] This quotation, incidentally, reveals Robert's weakness in his native tongue, which has led commentators to assume his schooling was brief, and confirms that, unlike his brothers, he never went to university. He may also possibly have been autistic.

Years later, when Robert was living in Spain, the English ambassador at Madrid, who knew both the brothers, wrote that he had a much higher opinion of Robert than of Anthony: 'Mr Sherley hath here gotten very great reputation; through his wise and discreet carriage he is judged both modest and moreover brave in his speech, diet and expenses, and in my poor opinion, to those vices which in Anthony do so abound, in this man may be found the contrary.'[3] But, as we shall shortly see, all this discretion and modesty did not help Robert in dealing with the enmity he encountered in Spain, and then in England. He turned out to be somewhat of a political innocent when up against ruthless opposition, and this quality of innocence perhaps shows up in his portraits.

Previously, it was believed that the Sherley brothers introduced gunpowder and cannon to the Persian armies. This was partly due to Samuel Purchas writing in 1625. However, it is clear the Persians possessed both cannons and muskets long before the arrival of the Sherleys (see Appendix I). Also, it is difficult to see how Anthony could have achieved much in the way of military or technical reform, considering he was at the Persian royal court only a few months, and spoke neither Persian nor Turkish, the two languages of the court. Regarding Robert, he might well have accompanied the Shah on his various campaigns, along with Thomas Powell, who is described in one document as 'a gunner',[4] in which case both might have taken part in the actual fighting. This is what Abbas wrote in a letter to Cecil in 1607: 'He [Powell] hath been in the company of the worthy gentleman Robert Sherley in all the actions, sieges, and battles that we have had against the Turks, and hath done us in those wars great service.'[5] In spite of this commendation, one has to remember that Robert himself, unlike Anthony, lacked any previous military experience.

At the start of his stay in Persia, which was to last nearly nine years, Robert was well looked after, receiving a regular income from the Shah. However, as the years passed and Anthony did not return from Europe, Robert's status at the Persian court seems to have deteriorated somewhat. In a letter to his brother he writes: 'As for myself, I cannot denie, but he giveth me still the same meanes he was wont: but God knowes yt is in such a Scurvie fashion that I cannot possible meynteine myself with yt, and it is ery yeare *da mal in peggio* [from bad to worse].'

This letter, written in 1605, is one of two from Robert to his brother which have survived, presumably because they were seized by agents on their way to Anthony. But with these two we have enough to show there must have been a regular correspondence between the brothers. For instance, Robert reproaches Anthony for so often making promises he does not fulfil: 'Your often promising to send presents, artificers, and Signor Angelo [Corrai] and I know not how many else, hath made me be esteemed a common liar; brother, for God's sake, either perform, or not promise anything.' The letters also show how unhappy Robert was at this time, and how much he would have liked to leave Persia: 'Dere brother, I am soe besids myself with the travailes and wants I am in, and the little hope I have of yor retorne or of anie helpe from my delivry out of the Countrie.'[6]

The negligent treatment of Robert by Abbas was probably due to his irritation that Anthony had not fulfilled his mission as ambassador, or come back to Persia. However, in early 1608 Robert heard from relatives in England about the Spanish king's choice of Anthony as admiral in charge of a fleet to protect Naples and Sicily against pirates. When the Shah was told this news, the status of the Sherley brothers must have risen in his eyes, which perhaps explains his dispatching Robert as his new ambassador to Europe the following year. Sometime before this appointment, Robert experienced two life-changing experiences: the first being his conversion to the Catholic faith, which possibly had taken place sometime earlier and may have been through the influence of the Augustinian priest, Antonio de Gouveau. The second was in February 1608, when he married Sampsonia, the eighteen-year-old daughter of a Christian Circassian nobleman. She, too, was baptised as a Roman Catholic and was given the name Teresia. She was to accompany Robert during most of his future travels, and saved his life at least once. When he died she went to live in Rome, from where she organised the transport of his body from Istahan for burial in her parish church in Rome. Before Robert's marriage, Thomas Powell had also married a Persian lady, Tomasin.

Robert set off with Powell and their two wives early in 1608. They journeyed across the Caspian Sea to Russia, and then by land to Poland where Robert temporarily left Teresia in a convent before travelling to Prague, and then south to Florence and Rome. Everywhere he went he was treated with the respect he felt was his due as an ambassador. His journey ended in Madrid where he met King Philip III and his leading minister, the Duke of Lerma. According to his instructions from Abbas, he offered them a highly profitable monopoly in Persian silk, and the opening of a new trade route via Hormuz and the Cape of Good Hope which would bypass Turkish territory. In return he asked that Spain declare war against Turkey, suggesting an attack on Cyprus and then perhaps Aleppo.

At first Robert's proposals were received politely, and he was given a handsome pension to live on while in Spain. He sent a message to Teresia asking her to join him while he awaited confirmation of his proposals, which she did. However, as long months passed and he heard nothing positive he became disillusioned, and early in 1610 he confided his doubts to Francis Cottington, the English ambassador in Madrid. Cottington was impressed by Robert, but could do little to help him. He wrote to Robert Cecil (now Lord Salisbury): 'I do not perceive that he is possessed with those vanities which do so much govern his brother Anthony. He is not pleased with his entertainment here. He tells me he resolves to go from hence directly into England, and that by kind letters received from your Lordship, he hath understood His Majesty is contented that he also perform his embassage there.'[7] It was soon after this that Robert met his brother Anthony who had just retired to Spain, having been relieved of his post as a Spanish admiral (see the next chapter). A final blow for Robert's hopes in Spain was when a Persian, also purporting to be an ambassador sent by Abbas, appeared in Madrid. This new arrival presented the king with a large present of Persian silk. He was hostile to Robert, and denied that he was really an ambassador at all. All this was too much for Robert, and with Teresia he finally said goodbye to Spain and made his way to England.

In August 1611, Robert arrived at Wiston to what must have been a sad meeting with his parents. Old Sir Thomas was bankrupt, expecting to have to give up his ancestral mansion at any moment in order to meet his debts. He was also ill, and was to die within a few months. Robert's elder brother, Thomas, was deeply in debt, and his other brother, Anthony, was living in Granada, subsisting on a small pension from the king of Spain. Robert and his pregnant wife, Teresia, stayed at Wiston for a month, during which time Robert wrote to Cecil begging him to arrange for the debt collectors to postpone their action since, 'my father at this present beinge very sick is exceedingly trobled in his mynde about a seasure wch he feareth will shortly come upon him, and all his Tennants in respect of an arrerage of Rent wch he sayeth is due from him to the King's Majesty.'[8] This petition was successful, and the old man was allowed to end his days in his ancestral home.

The new young ambassador had a series of meetings with King James I which went fairly well, once the king had got over the idea of one of his subjects appearing as the agent of a foreign power, and wearing a Persian turban. James seemed interested in the idea of England becoming the hub of the silk trade, receiving raw silk from Persia and reselling it throughout Europe. He even considered investing personally in this new venture, along with any independent gentlemen who might want to join in. Salisbury, the king's leading minister, was also not unfavourable to Robert's suggestions. Robert got to know King James's wife, Anne, and his older son, Prince Henry, who at the age of nearly nineteen was beginning to interest himself in England's foreign policies.

However, the powerful merchants of both the Levant company and the East India Company were totally opposed to everything Robert suggested, sure that their existing trade with Turkey would be badly affected. As the political commentator John Chamberlain wrote, '[Sherley] hath had divers audiences, but I doubt his projects are to little purpose, for the way is long and dangerous, the trade uncertain, and must quite cut off our traffic with the Turk.'[9] Meanwhile, Teresia had her baby, a son who was christened Henry after Prince Henry, who had agreed to be the baby's sponsor at the baptism. Robert's letter to the prince requesting this favour demonstrates his usual weakness when it came to spelling:

> Most renownede Prince. The great honnors and favors it hathe pleased your highnes to use towards me hathe imbowldede me to wright thes fewe lyns, wich shal be to beseeehe your highnes to Cristen a son wich God hathe given me. Your highnes in this shal make your servant happy, whos whole londginge is to doe your highnes som segnniolated servis, worthy to be esteemed in your Prinsly brestt. I have not the pen of Sissero, yett wontt I not means to sownde your highnesses worthy prayses in to the ears of forran nattions and migtey Prinses; and I assure myselfe,

your highborne sperritt thirstes after fame, the period of greate Prinses ambisions; and further, I will ever be your highnes most humbele.[10]

All Robert's plans came to nothing when Salisbury died in May 1612, and Prince Henry in November the same year. King James now turned to a series of incompetent favourites to help him rule the country, and his interest in Persian silk waned. Robert's father also died the same year, and James gave Wiston to his first favourite courtier, Robert Carr, Earl of Somerset. With little to hope for, Robert decided to return to Persia, which he did together with Teresia, leaving behind the baby to be looked after in the Queen's household. Captain Powell and his wife and brother accompanied the Sherleys, along with others.[11]

Their ship was to proceed to the Far East, so a suitable place was looked for along the south coast of Persia where Sherley's party could be dropped. Gwadar (in what today is Pakistan) was chosen, where the natives seemed very friendly, but were actually plotting to kill the whole group once they disembarked, and then seize the ship. The plot was discovered in the nick of time, and Robert had no alternative but to sail on towards India, a decision that was to delay their arrival at Isfahan for more than a year.

They finally left the ship at Diul Sinde, a now vanished port at the mouth of the Indus river not far from Karachi. Unfortunately, this place turned out to be full of Portuguese and their supporters who treated the travellers badly. They tried to escape, only to be brought back by soldiers sent by the governor of Diul Sinde who was in thrall to the Portuguese. Overcome by the stress of their situation, Robert now became ill and took to his bed. One night Portuguese soldiers set fire to the house he and his wife were renting, and only Teresia's determination rescued him from his sick bed and pulled him from the burning building. Captain Powell was killed in this incident, and shortly afterwards his Persian wife died as well. Eventually, the Sherleys did escape, with some other Englishmen, to make their way across the Indian countryside to Agra to seek justice from Jahangir, the Moghul emperor, who received them courteously and ordered the governor of Diul Sinde to be punished.

After a few months at Jahangir's court, Robert and Teresia left for Isfahan where they arrived in March 1615, over two years after leaving England. By this time Shah Abbas's plans were going well. After defeating the Turks he had signed a peace treaty with them, and was now considering whether this was a good moment for attacking the Portuguese base at Hormuz and taking away their monopoly of Eastern trade. To do this he needed cooperation with a maritime power such as England, since Persia lacked naval power. Because he had been impressed with Robert's previous trip as ambassador, Abbas now decided to send him back again to Europe to seek alliances and offer trade. One of his motives was to reassure the Spanish, although secretly preparing his attack on Hormuz. Robert reluctantly agreed to go back to Spain, while trying to keep the details of his mission secret from the Portuguese.

In October 1615, Robert and Teresia left Isfahan for the second time. The plan was to reach Goa, and from there take a Portuguese ship round the Cape and to Lisbon. But when they got to Goa they found they had just missed the annual fleet which sailed to Lisbon, and they had to spend a year waiting for the next one. Finally, they reached Lisbon and went on to Madrid. Robert's instructions were to suggest to Philip III much the same deal as he had offered four years earlier: an advantageous trade in Persian silk coupled with a Spanish promise to attack the Ottoman Empire. However, the result was also the same. Robert was treated well, befitting his status as an ambassador, but the King and his ministers prevaricated, and months and then years passed with discussions, proposals, frustrations, and no real progress. Most probably, the Spanish had grasped that Robert's visit was a smokescreen to hide projected events in the Persian gulf. Eventually he became disillusioned and decided to leave Spain, proceeding first to Holland, with much the same result as in Spain, then to Rome (where he and Teresia had their portraits painted by van Dyck), and eventually to England.

Robert arrived in England in December 1623, and remained there five years. For much of the time he stayed with his sister Mary, who had married Sir John Crofts and lived near Newmarket in Suffolk. He had to deal with a highly complex situation. On the one hand, James I was still well disposed towards his offer that London could become the staple for the export of Persian silk to the rest of Europe. On the other, the City of London, dominated by the Levant and East India Companies, was against his proposals. Levant merchants, whose trade was through Aleppo and other Ottoman cities, felt sure that the Turks would react to Sherley's new silk trade with hostility and ruin their existing trade. East India Company merchants, while interested in a new trade in Persian silk, were suspicious of Sherley, asking why he had spent so long negotiating with the Spanish before coming to England. The merchants spread all kinds of derogatory rumours about him: that he was not a real ambassador, that he had no authority to offer trade deals, that he had become a Moslem while in Persia, that his wife was a harlot. They went so far as to request Shah Abbas to send another ambassador to England to clarify matters, and that they would meet all his expenses. Abbas, who was never averse to sending off ambassadors, sent a Persian named Nuqd Ali Beg who, as soon as he arrived, proclaimed that Sherley was indeed an imposter, and that his credentials were forgeries.

When a meeting was arranged between the two ambassadors and some of their supporters, there occurred an unexpectedly violent scene as described by an observer. Robert was holding in his hand his letters from the Shah when suddenly Nuqd Ali Beg, 'rising out of his chaire, stept to Sir Robert Sherley, snatcht his Letters from him, toare them, and gave him a blow on the face with his Fist, and while my Lord of Cleveland stepping between kept off the offer of a further violence; the Persians son next at hand flew upon Sir Robert Sherley, and with two or three blows more, overthrew him.' Robert, in a state of shock, then retreated behind his friends, and the observer of the scene makes this comment: 'The greatest blot was cast upon Sir Robert Sherley for his default in his resolution not to return with blows (or words at least) the affront done to him; which had he done, would have confirmed the truth of his representative quality, and not given subject (from such weaknesse and want of spirit) to the Merchants to dispute (as they confidently did) and to his own friends to defend the soundness of his commission.'[12]

A few months before this altercation Robert had suffered yet another setback. King James died, and his son Charles, who succeeded him (his older son, Henry, having died in 1612), seemed less interested in developing the Persian silk trade. Arguments continued between the two ambassadors and their factions, but Robert clearly saw that the game was lost. Charles, who had been irritated by Nuqd Ali Beg's behaviour, now decided on a compromise. Robert and his rival would return to Persia and request the Shah to decide between them. The East India Company would transport the two ambassadors, and would be recompensed if it turned out that Sherley was a fraud. The EIC was not keen on this arrangement, but finally Robert set off on one of their ships accompanied by Sir Dodmore Cotton, whom Charles sent as ambassador to explain matters to Abbas.

After many delays, mainly due to the company's reluctance to receive Robert on board one of their ships, the three of them, Robert, Dodmore Cotton and Nuqd Ali Beg, set off for Persia by way of the Cape. Several other gentlemen accompanied them, including Sir Thomas Herbert who was to write an account of their journey. Robert, his wife, Teresia, and Cotton were placed in a different ship from Nuqd Ali Beg in case there was further violence between them. Shortly before arrival, however, the latter killed himself with an overdose of opium, probably because he knew what the Shah's reaction would be when he was told all the facts.

The group had a long and difficult journey, first to the East India Company base at Surat north of Mumbai, and then by another ship to Shah Abbas's new trading base at Bandar Abbas at the entrance to the Persian Gulf (Abbas having by this time driven the Portuguese from nearby Hormuz). From there they went across Persia to Ashref on the Caspian Sea where Robert had his first, and only, interview with the Shah. They then had to follow Abbas across the mountains to Qazvīn. By now Robert knew he was out of favour, because it had become clear to the Shah that this, his second mission as ambassador, like his first, had failed to achieve anything. He was also ill from the journey, but he tried to improve the situation with a meeting with the Shah's chief minister, Muhammed Ali Beg. However, this meeting was to lead to disaster. The minister told him that he suspected his letter of credence from Abbas, presumably salvaged from the violence of Nuqd Ali Beg two years earlier, was possibly forged, and asked if he could show it to the Shah.

A few days later the minister announced that he had shown the letter to Abbas who had flown into a rage because it was a forgery, and had torn it to pieces. Clearly, Robert was being cheated and the letter had not been shown to Abbas at all, but by now he was too ill and tired to protest. Within a few weeks he died, broken-hearted at his treatment by a king to whose service he had dedicated his life. His friends buried his body beside the house in Qazvīn where he had been living. Not long afterwards his companion diplomat, Dodmore Cotton, also died, of dysentery, and the rest of the mission were left to make their own way home as best they could. Thomas Herbert summed up his view of Robert's character and the way he had been treated: 'From the Persian monarch he obtained least when he best deserved, and most expected it. His condition was free, noble, but inconstant. He was the greatest Traveller in his time, and had tasted liberally of many great Princes favours. His patience was better than his intellect, he was not much acquainted with the Muses, but what he wanted in Phylosophy, hee supplyed in Languages. Rank me with those that honour him.'[13]

The postscript to this sad story is that Teresia Sherley was not treated well while in Persia, but later managed to escape to Rome, where she lived for many years before her death in 1668. Some years before she died she arranged for Robert's body to be transported to Rome and buried in her local church, Santa Maria della Scala in Trastevera, where there is still today a plaque in Latin to husband and wife. In English it reads:

> To God, most good, most great.
> Robert Sherley, most noble Englishman, Emperor Rudolf's Count, his knight entitled to wear ornaments of gold, Ambassador of Shah Abbas, King of Persia. At the behest of the Roman Pontiff, renowned orator to the Emperor, to the Kings of Spain, England, Poland, Muscovy, Morocco [Confusion here with Anthony?], and to other European Princes.
>
> Theresia Sampsonia, native of the region of the Amazons, daughter of Samphuffus, Prince of Circassia. For her most beloved husband, the resting place of herself and the bones of her husband who died in Persia and whose bones were brought to this city by herself in her twenty-ninth year, 1668.[14]

Chapter 17

Peso Politico

By 1611 Sir Anthony's public career was over. He was now deeply in debt, and from Granada he made his way to Madrid to plead his cause with the King. Here he was welcomed by his brother Robert who had just arrived from Persia on his first voyage as an ambassador. The Sherleys had not seen each other for over a decade, and Robert invited Anthony to stay in his house. The English ambassador in Madrid, Francis Cottington, reported that Sir Anthony was 'extremely poor both in purse and reputation, which he well perceives, and talks sometimes of his going to England, and sometimes of a journey into Persia with his brother.'[1]

The brothers got on well at first, but about two months later Robert was shocked to discover that Anthony had been plotting with the Spanish authorities to prevent him travelling to England. 'Oh Mr. Cottington,' Robert told the English ambassador, 'I am betrayed where I am most trusted.' Robert showed Cottington a letter from the Spanish King's secretary to Anthony which said, 'I have given an account to his Majesty of your plot, by which the Ambassador your brother may be secured from proceeding with his intention of going into England, who commands me to give you thanks in his name, and to let you know how well he takes your endeavours.'[2] In spite of Anthony's attempt to stop him, Robert did manage to leave for England; Anthony stayed a few months longer in Madrid in considerable poverty. The English ambassador reported: 'He hath scarce money to buy him bread and is lodged in a Bodegon, which is little worse than an English ale house.'[3]

Eventually Sherley went back to Granada where, apart from brief visits to other parts of Spain, he was to spend the rest of his life, living off his small government pension. He continued to suggest various ambitious schemes to the Spanish authorities, and some of them were discussed by the King's Council of State, though none of them were actually implemented. For instance, he advised blocking the East India

Company's port of Surat by sinking four ships loaded with stone in the narrow entrance to the harbour in order to damage English trade with India and the Far East. And when, in 1617, it was rumoured that Sir Walter Raleigh was planning a voyage to the Orinoco in search of the fabled gold of El Dorado, Sherley was invited to give his advice as to how to intercept him. He made his proposals, adding, 'If I am acceptable for the carrying out of this task, I offer my life and labour for it, or alternatively I will serve in Poland, Milan or on any duty that His Majesty may command'. In a plaintive conclusion he added, 'But if I am of no use for any service, it seems to me to be unreasonable that His Majesty should give me such an ample salary.'[4] On another occasion he suggested that he should be given the island of Capri, which he would make into a centre for the sale of Spanish products throughout the Mediterranean.[5] No such offers were taken up.

In 1613 Sherley tried a different way of making money. The English ambassador noted that he 'hath now great hopes by a copper mine which he hath discovered and procured a grant from this King, and truly I am informed it may prove a matter of great consequence. He hath for divers months past lived in a town called Veza [Baeza] near unto his mine in the Kingdom of Granada where he hath 3,000 ducats per annum very punctually paid him, and never lived so well or orderly as at this present.'[6] Nothing more, however, is heard of this project, so the mine may not have been as productive as first hoped. Nevertheless, the King's ministers continued to listen to Sherley and pay some attention to his proposals. One of them, while refusing a suggestion by Sherley that he be allowed to settle in Spanish America, commented, 'In the meantime we should not lose sight of this gentleman whom I could use under a capable leader who knew how to utilize his good qualities without paying attention to his speeches.'[7]

During Sherley's life Spain had seen many changes. The Union of the Crowns (1580-1640) meant that Portugal and Spain became in effect one nation under the Spanish monarch. Portugal's Asian trade through its ports of Goa on the west coast of India, and Hormuz at the entrance to the Persian Gulf, now formed part of the worldwide Spanish Empire. But in 1598 the capable and hard-working Philip II died, to be succeeded by a less dedicated monarch, his son Philip III, who was inclined to leave the details of government to his favourite minister, the Duke of Lerma, while he pursued his personal pleasures such as hunting, bullfights and

Peso Politico

ceremonial processions. During the twenty years of Lerma's rule he and his friends became richer while the rest of the nation steadily declined. An extravagant and corrupt court supported a growing class of nobles who relied on government hand-outs and were disinclined to work. Peasants and craftsmen were over-taxed, so that farming suffered and whole villages became depopulated. Spanish industry, particularly the manufacture of textiles, could not compete with increasing imports of foreign goods. Gold and silver from the Americas tended to disappear en route to the royal coffers, and the currency declined in value. The Spanish army, which under Philip II had been the best in Europe, went downhill, and the navy could hardly cope with the need to police the enlarged empire.

In 1621 Philip III died, to be succeeded by his sixteen-year-old son as Philip IV. The following year Sherley composed a book entitled *Peso Politico de todo el mundo* (*The Political Balance of the Whole World*) which he dedicated to Gaspar de Guzmán, Duke of Olivares, whom he knew was about to become the new King's leading minister.[8] This chapter is not so much about the Anthony Sherley who died in relative poverty in a remote part of Spain, or whose suggestions were largely ignored by the Spanish authorities. Rather, it is about Sherley as the author of this book, whom one historian has described as a visionary[9], and about the book itself, concerning which another historian wrote: '*Sans aucun doute,* le Peso Politico *restera l'un des exemples les plus curieux et les plus significatifs de la littérature politique de cette époque.*'[10] As its title implies, this was a highly ambitious work, in which Sherley considered, nation by nation, the strengths and weakness of each, and how they affected each other, seeing them all as interlinking cogs in what he called 'the machine of the world'. He ends with advice to Olivares as to how to reform Spain, and especially her foreign policies. The book has been relatively neglected, and has never been translated into English from Sherley's Spanish.

Here, Sherley uses his wide first-hand knowledge of different countries. Presumably, for places he had never visited he recalled the views of people he had once met, or used whatever books he had to hand in Granada. His remit goes far beyond Europe. For instance, about China under the Ming dynasty he concludes that 'it is a very great empire extended over an enormous territory, and plentiful in everything that is necessary for life and its enjoyment; the sole serious problem is that its military is made up of uninterested peasants and that it has no access to horses of good quality.'[11] At this time other authors, too, were giving their views on how to improve Spain's worsening status in the world, but compared to many of them Sherley seems relatively objective, and hence surprisingly modern in tone. For instance, the philosopher and diplomat Giovanni Botero, who died in 1617, rendered advice to the Spanish government from the position of a committed Catholic who saw not only Protestant nations as heretical but also the entire Moslem world as infidels, and hence potential enemies. He explained that Western nations were civilised and subject to the rule of law, while those in the East, such as Turkey and Persia, were one and all ruthless dictatorships.

Sherley, on the other hand, was less interested in particular religions or even in dictatorships (though these are mentioned where appropriate). Instead, he concentrates on the economic, political and military potential of a particular nation. He uses the term 'substance' to describe how far a nation was self-sufficient in essential commodities, and how far it might be weakened by having to rely on foreign trade. He said, for instance, that the power of England was 'limited by the size of the kingdom, and all the remaining breadth that it has acquired is through exchange, and since on its own it does not have the substance to carry out or sustain those exchanges, once one knows their secret they can be cut off or at least restricted with the application of a little care to do so.' But the Spanish Empire, he claimed, had that 'unique quality that no other state possesses in that all the necessary materials are native to them and are a part of this Monarchy, which does not need to acquire anything [from outside].' Therefore its present 'ills and weaknesses' can easily be cured 'once one has knowledge of the substances of all the other nations, and one is certain of one's own substance.'

About Persia, there is no mention of Sherley's former close relationship with Shah Abbas. In the political balance of the world he rates Turkey as far more powerful in the long run, even though Persia's scorched earth policy sometimes brings military success: 'The Persian is a powerful potentate but most unequal to the Turk, and though his militia is good it cannot compare to the Turkish one. The war he makes on the Turk is not a war of equal power, but rather of periodic attacks, laying waste to whole provinces to deprive the Turkish army of all sorts of supplies. Nor can the Persian retain what he has won from the Turk for any more time than is needed for the general government of the Turkish empire to

Peso Politico

recover from its infirmities.' Sherley finds that a lack of 'substance' is the ultimate cause of Persia's military weakness: 'Finally this kingdom, though it has much in abundance, lacks an even greater number of things, and it has one of the greatest weaknesses that an empire can have; and that is that it has a sea front and no force on the sea, nor does it possess the possibility of having any such force for lack of wood.'

To say that the *Peso Politico* is relatively objective is not to overlook some of Sherley's prejudices acquired from past experiences. For example, he has this to say about Russia, where he had been held against his will for several months during his journey from Persia to the West. He starts off with some objective details:

> Their religion is Greek but very adulterated, and despite not being well-inclined to any other sect than their own, they do get along with heretics [i.e. Protestants]. Foodstuffs of all sorts abound, and they have it extremely cheap. The Prince is the absolute and despotic lord of all lives and goods. Their militia [army] is made up of cavalry and infantry. The cavalry uses the same arms as the Tartars: bows, scimitars and maces, but few lances and leather shields. The infantry is more or less made up of bowmen, with a few harquebuses that are three palms and less.

At this point, however, he gives vent to his personal feelings about Russians: 'They are a false people, with neither law nor word, malicious, suspicious and so given to drinking that from nine in the morning to the next day one cannot have trade or dealings with them; lying and most cruel, but so subject to their Princes that they could be called bestially obedient.'

Another state of which Sherley had bitter memories, where he was imprisoned twice and then forced to leave, was Venice, which, he writes, 'calls itself a republic, but under the name of liberty is really the most tyrannical state there is or has been, and keeps up the name as an artifice in order to mislead all princes.'

One feature of the *Peso Politico* is Sherley's attempt to integrate into his description of different nations, episodes from the past, and from his own life. He has, for instance, a lot to say about the English attack on Cádiz in 1596, which was ultimately unsuccessful, partly due to rivalry between its two leaders, Essex and Howard. Sherley claimed he had special knowledge that the real object of this expedition was not just to destroy Spanish ships preparing for a new armada (as most histories of the period say), but also to capture Cádiz and keep it as a permanent base from which to harass Spanish trade with the Americas.[12] Another of these digressions into history was the one in which Sherley alleged that he himself had been selected by the Earl of Leicester, towards the end of 1586, to carry a faked letter from Mary, Queen of Scots to the Spanish general in the Netherlands, the Duke of Parma, proposing that the two of them get married and then seize the throne of England (see also chapter 2).[13]

Very likely, this last story was apocryphal; perhaps Sherley invented it to remind Olivares that he was not a mere armchair advisor but someone who had himself been a major player in recent history. In another passage he emphasises his credentials as a traveller of the world, comparing himself favourably in this respect with even the great Machiavelli and those who imitated him: 'Others take out a poultice of rules from Machiavelli's pouch, not realizing that he was only the secretary of the tiny republic of Florence, and as his science was born within such narrow walls ... his blinkered vision could not carry the early seventeenth century theorist of world affairs very far.'

The most important part of the *Peso Politico*, for Olivares as well as for Sherley, must have been the advice it offered on how to improve Spain's position in the world. Here, his outstanding recommendation was that a pact should be formed between the Spanish and Ottoman empires. This is startling when one remembers that twenty years earlier Sherley had been an ambassador for Shah Abbas, sent to persuade the leading European nations to form an alliance with Persia so that the hated Turks could be attacked from every side. Now, however, he argues that Spain and Turkey had much in common; their governments were similar, they shared common enemies, and they were easily the leading powers in the world. To explain what their relationship should be he employs an astrological metaphor which would have been easily understood by his contemporary readers:

> It seems to me that effectively there are only two great planets in the matter of domination, of which this Monarchy as the larger one is the sun, and the Turk's empire is the

moon. And as it is inevitable that the sun of this Monarchy, on account of the passage of time, will make its way through many zodiac signs, some of which will heat it up more than others, it is the wisest course to arrange everything in such a way that it is not eclipsed through opposition with the moon, from which many evils and perilous and pernicious effects will always follow.[14]

Sherley realised that such a pact, after decades of hostility, might need considerable diplomacy to bring about. He said it should be made to appear as if the initiative came from Turkey rather than Spain. Then he suggests that there was really only one man capable of negotiating such an arrangement: 'and this I could do, and without arrogance may say that no other has the capacity or understands the methods required to make such a treaty.'

An agreement with Turkey would allow Spain to concentrate on her real enemies which were England and Holland, whose commercial energy threatened Spain's global domination. Here Sherley turned to ways of undermining the trade of these northern nations. He suggests methods for reviving the Spanish textile industry, including taxes on imported foreign cloth, and also how to revive both the Asian spice trade and the sale of goods from the Americas by setting up industrial fairs, especially in Italy, so as to attract foreign merchants. Another proposal was a permanent blockade of the Straits of Gibraltar to prevent English and Dutch merchants from entering the Mediterranean. This aggressive move had been discussed earlier, but Sherley was perhaps unaware that Olivares had actually tried it the year before he was sent the *Peso Politico*. A fleet of seventy-six vessels had been set up by the Spanish, of which eighteen were to patrol the Straits at any given time, but apparently even this had failed to prevent access by enemy merchant ships.

Did Olivares actually read Sherley's book? There is no direct evidence that he did, and certainly his policies as leading minister over the next twenty-two years show little evidence that he took up Sherley's main suggestions. He certainly never made overtures for an alliance with the Ottoman Turks. His time was a period of almost constant war, and he tried, but failed, to halt Spain's steady economic decline. On the other hand, we are told he was a man of letters, and that he owned a large library full of works on history and geography. According to the historian

John Elliott, who wrote a biography of Olivares, 'the Count Duke was probably the first ruler of the Spanish monarchy to think in genuinely global terms, and it is no accident that he should have felt at home with that bold adventurer Anthony Sherley, who would spin the globe with confidence and offer to reveal the secret strengths and weaknesses of every kingdom and sultanate between the Danish Sound and the coasts of Malabar.'[15]

Even after sending the *Peso Politico* to Olivares, Anthony continued to make new proposals to the Spanish authorities. I quote from David Davies who summarises a document from the Spanish archives at Simancas, in order to illustrate the typical complexity of Sherley's proposals. In this document there is a rare mention of Anthony's son, Diego:

> Two years later [i.e. in 1626, when Sherley was sixty-one] he put forward his most ambitious proposal, which was that he and his Spanish descendants, his son Don Diego is mentioned specifically, should be given proprietary rights to a town on the island of Fadala and another in Anafa, or Mogador, in Barbary [i.e. islands off the coast of Morocco], to hold as vassals of the King of Spain with the title of Señorio, or Seigneur, or Lord. He and his descendants would have the right to fortify these towns, to develop the fishery in the vicinity, to buy wheat, hides, meat, and other products in Barbary, and to sell these products in Spain. In return for these privileges Sherley agreed to maintain a fleet of fifty ships which would be at the disposal of the King four months of the year, and in the other eight months might be used by the Conde de Leste [Count of the East, a title which Sherley had awarded himself] in his trading operations. He was also to give the crown 60,000 ducats as a guarantee that he would carry out the arrangement and would not inflict damage on any of the King's subjects, friends, or allies.[16]

The guaranteed sum, however, was never produced, and the project seems to have evaporated without trace.

In 1633 a local chronicle in Granada published a slightly inaccurate obituary of Sir Anthony:

> In this year there died in this city the valorous knight, the Conde de Leste, the Englishman who sacked the city of Cádiz in the time of the King Philip II, though he did so against his will, for later he took refuge in Spain and his Majesty aided him with some revenues on silk in this said city of Granada, where he lived not very prosperously. His body was buried in the parish church of St Peter and St Paul in this city. He left a son with good qualities whom his Majesty will take into his service, for he is so capable in all matters.[17]

So here we have to say good bye to Sir Anthony Sherley, Conde de Leste, a man who fashioned himself not one identity, but several: soldier, privateer, ambassador, spy, nobleman, and finally, authority on the state of the world. A man who consorted with monarchs, whose charisma impressed the powerful, and who, even during his forced retirement, 'would spin the globe with confidence'. And mostly he achieved all this alone, without the support and backing of family, religion, or native land. Sir Anthony may not have changed the course of history much, as his one-time leader, Shah Abbas, certainly did, but his own personal history is surely compelling enough.

Conclusion

Over the centuries, opinions about Sir Anthony Sherley have varied enormously. Many of his contemporaries took him at his word, that he was a noble gentleman who lived for honour and who brought great advantages to his family and his country. Modern historians, who have found more material about him in the archives, are not so sure. According to Sir Dennison Ross, 'he must have possessed great physical courage and a reckless love of adventure,' and 'when reading his life we are carried away by his dominating personality.' However, 'he was an inveterate and unscrupulous intriguer, a sententious hypocrite devoid of any real sentiment, being incapable of single-minded devotion to any person or cause.'[1] The verdict of Boies Penrose is much the same: while 'he must have been rather a forceful and persuasive character,' yet 'he was a self-seeking adventurer pure and simple, a born intriguer, a complete opportunist.'[2] While not disagreeing with these assessments, I have tried to produce some explanation as to why it was that (going back to Ross) Sir Anthony 'passed without compunction or regret from one employment to another and surely it is seldom that one man has served so many masters.' I have listed the various external factors which ruined his later career: his bitter rivalry with the Persian whom Shah Abbas chose to accompany him to Europe; the fall and execution of his patron, Essex; the anger of Queen Elizabeth at his Persian mission, which led to her refusal to allow him back to his own country. While certainly not arguing that Sir Anthony was ever an admirable character, I think these factors show why he had little alternative after the failure of his embassy but to go 'from one employment to another,' and also they explain why, according to Penrose, 'from 1600 onward his character seemed to change rapidly for the worse.' To put it as politely as possible, he then chose to live by a more limited and highly personal concept of honour.

As the American historian, David Davies, who spent months and years pursuing the three Sherley brothers through foreign archives, admits towards the conclusion of his book: 'one must inevitably ask oneself if the story of the Sherleys is important, and the answer is, of course, that it is not. These men shaped no great moments in history.'[3] But Davies goes on to explain that history not only concerns important changes in society, politics or economics, but is also about individuals in the past – how they organised their lives, their assumptions, aspirations and achievements, and naturally, also, their failures.

The Sherley brothers, not to mention their father, did a lot of failing between them, and the various ways in which they failed are interesting, I think, and tell us much, not only about themselves, but also about their times. Historical generalisations, of course, have their place, but reading about the lives of particular people is more fun, and possibly just as important for us, since they were human beings too, and therefore have a lot to teach us. As Niall Ferguson has pointed out, the current world population makes up only seven per cent of all those who have ever lived, 'and we ignore the accumulated experience of such a huge majority of mankind at our peril.'[4] Someone might argue here that an imaginative historical novel can tell us more about selected individuals than any history book, with its inevitable gaps, possibly could. The trouble with historical novels, however, is that they rely on the imagination of the author to fill in those gaps. They are mostly made up, and therefore misleading for a keen student of history. (Having said that, I do think there is a fascinating novel about the Sherleys waiting to be written.) Here, I have done my best to stick to the facts – or rather, to 'facts' mentioned in letters from the archives, and/or cited by previous historians.

Talking of gaps reminds me of two related problems that anyone trying to write about people who lived four centuries ago must encounter. The first is that surviving records are mostly about men, and not women. The lives of the Sherleys exemplify this problem to a high degree. We know practically nothing about Anthony's relations with women – only that he left his young wife to go to sea after two years of marriage, and never saw her again. Also that years later, when he was living in Spain, he had a son with him named Diego. Nothing else. His brothers are not much better. Robert had a somewhat exotic wife called Teresia who accompanied him on most of his travels, and once saved his life by pulling him from a burning building. And Thomas had two wives in succession, and eighteen children.

The second problem concerning people from that period in history is linked to the first. It is that their personal feelings are usually no concern of the surviving documents, and are therefore hidden from us. Anthony can certainly express emotion when writing, for instance, to Essex, Queen Elizabeth or Robert Cecil. He wrote to Cecil from Archangel that the light in the eyes of the Queen was for him the fairest light in the world, and that all his adventures had only been 'to do some extraordinary thing which might honour Her Majesty's most excellent person.' He wrote to Essex at the same time about 'the fulness of my affection signed with that hand which no thing nor cause between heaven and earth shall ever alter.' The trouble is, of course, that the more he says, the less we believe him.

In spite of these gaps in our knowledge I think we know enough of Sir Anthony's life and career to agree with the French historian I mentioned in my introduction that he was '*cet étrange et bizarre personnage*', and, though to a lesser extent, so were his two brothers and also old Sir Thomas, their father. But the monarch who employed Anthony as a Persian ambassador, Shah Abbas the Great, was not at all bizarre, but rather, ambitious, ruthless and highly successful.

Appendix I

Doubtful stories associated with the Sherleys

(a) that Anthony and Robert Sherley taught the Persians how to use gunpowder, thus allowing them to defeat their enemies, the Turks.
Samuel Purchas (c.1577-1626), who succeeded William Hakluyt as publisher of reports by travellers to foreign countries, popularised this claim:

> And, finally, the mighty Ottoman, terror of the Christian world, quaketh of a Sherley fever, and gives hopes of approaching fates. The prevaling Persian hath learned Sherleian Arts of War, and he which before knew not the use of ordnance hath now 500 peeces of Brasse, and 60,000 Musketiers, so that they which at hand with the sword were before dreadful to the Turkes, now also in remoter blows and sulfurial arts are grown terrible.[1]

Until relatively recently, it was accepted that the Sherleys made important changes to Persia's armed forces, including the use of gunpowder. For instance, Evelyn Shirley, in his book published in 1848, could still argue that 'the new corps of infantry which Abbas had raised probably owed their discipline to the counsel and aid of the two Sherleys and their military followers ... we are indeed told that they not only formed this force, but taught the Persians the use of artillery.'[2]

Contemporary historians, however, starting with Roger Savory, have shown 'there is abundant evidence, both in the European and the Persian sources, that the Persians were familiar with the use of artillery, and that Persian troops were equipped with hand-guns and skilled in their use, long before the time of Abbas I.'[3] Even the diarists of Sherley's own party admitted this. George Manwaring states that the Persians were already 'very expert in their pieces or muskets, for although there are some which have written now of late that they had not the use of pieces until our coming into the country, this much must I write to their praise, that I did never did see better barrels of muskets than I did see there; and the King hath, hard by his court at Aspahane, above two hundred men at work, only making of pieces.'[4] (On this issue, see also Chapter 16.

(b) that Will Kemp, the actor, who met Sir Anthony in Rome (or Venice) in about 1601, was related to Anne Kempe, the mother of the brothers.
Apparently, there actually was a meeting between Anthony Sherley and the actor and comedian, Will Kemp, though it took place in Rome, not Venice. The literary historian, Samuel Chew, discovered a reference to this meeting in a contemporary diary.[5] The parentage of Will Kemp (c.1560-c.1603) is unknown, but it has been conjectured that, despite his plebeian persona, he was linked in some way to the Kempes of Ollantighe, near Ashford in Kent, who were a Catholic gentry family. Sir Thomas Kempe (1517-1591) did indeed have a son named William, who was Anne Kempe's brother. However, the claim that he was the actor cannot be true, since this William Kempe was buried at Wye church on 27 March 1597. Nonetheless, this alleged connection might help explain the otherwise surprising story – dramatised in the play, *The Travailes of the Three English Brothers* (1607) – that when Will Kemp, the actor, was in Italy in 1601 he met Anthony Sherley whom he already knew well from earlier days in London. So were he and Sir Anthony somehow related? Perhaps Will Kemp did belong somewhere on the Ollantighe family tree, perhaps he was related to the Sherleys, if not Anthony's uncle, and perhaps, too, they both had earlier been part of the London theatrical scene (see also Chapter 12 for their meeting).

(c) that Sir Anthony wrote the plays we ascribe to William Shakespeare.
This was the opinion of the Rev Scott F. Surtees (1814-89). Surtees was Rector of Richmond in Yorkshire, and then, for ten years before his death in 1889, Vicar of Dinsdale, an attractive little village situated on either side of the River Tees. The reason he chose Dinsdale must have been because he had also inherited the lordship of the manor there, a position the Surtees family had held for generations. When not performing his vicarly (or lordship) duties, Surtees had time to pursue his interest in archaeology, and also to research and privately publish booklets on a

range of topics, mostly as controversial as possible. One was *Julius Caesar, did he cross the Channel?* (1866), in which he argues on literary and archaeological evidence that Caesar landed to invade Britain, not near Dover, but at Cromer in Norfolk.

The booklet we are concerned with here was *William Shakespeare of Stratford-on-Avon: His Epitaph Unearthed, and the Author of the Plays Run to Ground*, (1888), in which Surtees makes the case for Sir Anthony Sherley as the author of Shakespeare's plays. His reasons include that, unlike Shakespeare, Sir Anthony travelled widely through Europe and the East, and therefore had the experience and knowledge of countries, and of royal courts, revealed in the plays. Also, that Sherley's meeting with Will Kemp, the actor, in Venice or possibly Rome, adds weight to the argument, as does the fact that so many of Shakespeare's plays have a character named Antonio – clearly a hidden reference to their real author! Quite how Sir Anthony ever had the time to write all these plays remains unexplained.

Appendix II

Five authors

Five authors who wrote about the Sherleys have helped me with this book, and I owe a debt of gratitude to all of them. Going by the dates when their books were published, the earliest is Evelyn Philip Shirley (1812-1882 – Shirley spelt with an i), politician, historian and genealogist. He was directly descended from the prolific Robert Shirley, 1st Earl Ferrers (who was married twice and had twenty-seven children), and distantly related to the Sherleys of Wiston. Evelyn Shirley published two books about the history of his widespread family: *Stemmata Sherleiana*, (1841, revised in 1873) ; and *The Sherley Brothers,* (1848). It is the second of these that has been of most use to me, largely because it contains numerous letters written by, or to, the brothers, which he transcribed, mainly from the National Archives.

Evelyn Shirley's historical studies included research on the history of the estates he had inherited from his father, including 60,000 acres in County Monaghan, Ireland, and Ettingham Park near Stratford-on-Avon. He was a Tory MP, representing, at different times, Monaghan and Warwickshire South, and he amassed a huge library, said to consist of 3,000 volumes, mainly on history and genealogy.

My second author is Sir Edward Dennison Ross (1871-1940), orientalist and linguist. Ross was largely responsible for founding the School of Oriental Studies (now SOAS), as part of the University of London, and was its first director from 1916 to 1937. During his life he travelled extensively, especially in the East, and was said to be able to read forty-nine languages (certainly including Persian and Arabic, as well as Tibetan and several Indian languages).

In partnership with the publisher Routledge, and with the medieval historian Eileen Power as co-editor, Ross set up *The Broadway Travellers*, a series of books about travel and exploration. By the time he retired the series contained twenty-six volumes, among which was his own *Sir Anthony Sherley and his Persian Adventure*, (Routledge, 1933).

Five authors

This volume is especially useful for anyone interested in the Sherley brothers because it contains the full accounts written by three of Sherley's companions on his journeys to and from Persia: William Parry, Abel Pinçon and George Manwaring.

The third author is the American, Boies Penrose (1902-1976), member of an ancient and wealthy Philadelphian family. Boies derived his unusual forename from his uncle and namesake, Boies Penrose, who was a well-known Republican senator. Boies (the author) lived most of his life in Pennsylvania, but also partly in Nettlecombe, a small village near Taunton, Somerset. He wrote several books on exploration during the Tudor and Stuart period, the best known being *Travel and Discovery in the Renaissance, 1420-1620*, (The Wessex Press, Taunton, 1952). His first book was *The Sherleian Odyssey* (1938), in which he developed the narrative of the brothers' lives, as initiated by Shirley and Ross. The book starts with an unusually modest – though possibly tongue-in-cheek – preface: 'This foreword is here chiefly to save critics the trouble of reading the rest of the book ... The ensuing work is based on the available printed material relating to the Sherley family. Few original manuscript sources were used; while the author has never been to Persia and is wholly ignorant of Persian.' In spite of this disclaimer, Penrose is helpful because, not only is his book very readable, but also he transcribes in his footnotes a number of letters, some of which are not included by his predecessors.

For many years Penrose was chairman of the Historical Society of Pennsylvania as well as a member of the Royal Geographical Society of London. He travelled widely, collected books as well as rare wines and furniture, and was a frequent lecturer at colleges in the USA. Altogether, he seems to have lived an enjoyable and cultured existence on the fringes of academia.

Fourth in the list comes Samuel Claggett Chew (1888-1960), about whom one knows little, except that he was a professor at Bryn Mawr College, Pennsylvania, a prestigious liberal arts college for women. Chew was probably a professor of English Literature at Bryn Mawr, since his published works include books on Byron, Hardy and Swinburn. His most successful publication – it went through twenty-seven editions between 1937 and 1974 – was *The Crescent and the Rose: Islam and England during the Renaissance*, (Oxford University Press, New York,

1937), a tome of 550 pages, of which about a quarter concerns the Sherley brothers.

Chew's book is mainly about the impact of the Middle East, particularly Turkey and Persia, on Elizabethan and Stuart England, as reflected in contemporary literature. In the topics he chooses his breadth of reference is always impressive. He discusses in detail what was known about Mohammad, and about the differences between Sunnis and Shi'ites (which, in the case of Sherley and his companions was not much). Another section of the book looks at the impact of Islamic piracy on Mediterranean trade, and at the careers of well known pirates such as those Anthony Sherley tried to enlist when he was appointed 'Captain General of the Mediterranean Sea' by King Philip III of Spain.

The last, but certainly not the least, of my five authors is David William Davies (1908-1986) who published *Elizabethans Errant. The Strange Fortunes of Sir Thomas Sherley and His Three Sons*, (Cornell University Press, Ithaca, New York, 1967). This book was written before the internet got going, and it is all the more impressive that Davies was able to personally search archives in England, Scotland, Spain, Venice and Sicily, and discover many hitherto unknown documents about the Sherleys. His book is therefore almost too detailed, incorporating far more information than the other four mentioned above. His style is often ironic as he relates the faults of, and errors made by, Sir Thomas and his three sons.

Davies is said to have gained three PhDs – in History, Education, and Library Science. For much of his career he worked as a librarian in various institutions, ending up as chief librarian at the Central Library of the Claremont Colleges at Claremont, California. He often travelled to Europe, especially England, for research, accompanied by his wife, Thelma, and he joined the US army in the Second World War, when he trained as a cryptographer. Today, the Huntington Library near Los Angeles, California, holds fifteen boxes of his letters to Thelma, written while he was away in the army and she was in a tuberculosis sanatorium.

Appendix III

The uncertainty of letters

Sir Anthony was a prolific correspondent. Throughout his career abroad he wrote dozens of letters, especially to his friends and contacts at home. This was particularly the case when he still had hopes of returning to England. On his journey back from Persia in 1599-1600 he wrote from Moscow, from Archangel, from Emden in Germany, and from Prague. Many of his letters, or letters written to him, have long since disappeared. For instance, when his father wrote to him, thinking he was still in Persia, he referred to other letters which we do not now possess: 'I have four letters of yours,' old Sir Thomas wrote, 'which do import your filial regard to me and also your remorse towards me, whereof I take much comfort; so does your mother.'[1]

Some of Anthony's letters have survived because they never reached him, but were seized by Robert Cecil's agents, ending up in the Cecil Papers at Hatfield. In his account of the Sherley brothers, which includes many transcripts of letters, Evelyn Shirley wrote, 'We are obliged to the system of intercepting letters, from which indeed the great part of the materials of these memoirs are derived.'[2]

Seizure, however, did not necessarily mean that the person addressed in the letter never read it. They might have still received it if the writer had sent copies of the letter by several different paths. This was the case when Robert Sherley in Isfahan sent a letter to Anthony in September 1606. He wrote, 'You shal receive here inclosed a letter from His Majesty [Shah Abbas], the which I thought good to copy out, and send them by three conveyances, hoping that one of them unfeignedly will come to your hands.'[3]

Appendix IV

A portrait of Anthony Sherley?

There is a shortage of portraits of Sir Anthony, considering how famous he was during his career. In 1600-01, during the three months he spent in Prague visiting Emperor Rudolf II, the artist Aegidius Sadeler, Rudolf's court engraver, made line drawings of both him and Hussein Ali Beg, his Persian rival as ambassador. The one of Sir Anthony was subsequently copied, it seems, since the National Portrait Gallery has three line drawings of him, presumably by different artists, but all clearly based on Sadeler's original.

Apart from these drawings there is no portrait that can definitely be shown to be of Sir Anthony, a fact that caused me some concern until I came across an illustration in Boies Penrose's book, *The Sherleian Odyssey* (1938). This is an attractive painting of a young man in an armoured breastplate with his left hand resting beside his helmet on a table next to him. At the top right is written that the portrait was painted in 1588, and that the young man was twenty-three years old. This fits in well with what we know about Sir Anthony, who was born in 1565, and in 1588 may well have been home on leave during the time he was the youthful captain of a company, fighting the Spanish in the Netherlands. Penrose's caption to the portrait states:

SIR ANTHONY SHERLEY IN ARMOUR
From the painting by F. Zucchero
(Present whereabouts unknown)

This portrait, which is now held in the Metropolitan Museum in New York, was owned for over half a century by Charles Callis Western, 1st Baron Western, of Felix Hall and Rivenhall, Sussex, and his descendants. The family was connected by more than one marriage to the Sherleys of Wiston. In 1913 the Westerns sold this portrait at auction, naming it a portrait of Sir Anthony, but at some later stage

A portrait of Anthony Sherley?

it was described instead as a portrait of Sir John Shurley of Isfield, who married Anthony's sister, Jane. We know little of this Sir John, except that, unfortunately, he was born the same year as Anthony,[1] so the attribution is still under question. But I would like to believe that Lord Western and Boies Penrose were right, and that the young man in armour really was Sir Anthony Sherley.

Endnotes

References used in Endnotes

Cecil Papers	Cecil Papers, Hatfield, calendared in HMC Salisbury MSS.
CSP	Calendar of State Papers, National Archives.
ODNB	Oxford Dictionary of National Biography.
Blow	David Blow, *Shah Abbas: The Ruthless King Who Became an Iranian Legend,* I.B. Tauris, 2009.
Chew	Samuel Chew, *The Crescent and the Rose*, Oxford University Press, New York, 1937.
Davies	D.W. Davies, *Elizabethans Errant,* Cornell University Press, New York, 1967.
Don Juan	*Don Juan of Persia: A Shi`ah Catholic, 1560-1604,* trans. Guy le Strange, Routledge 1926.
Penrose	Boies Penrose, *The Sherleian Odyssey*, The Wessex Press, Taunton, 1938.
Relation	*Sir Anthony Sherley, His Relation of his Travels into Persia*, 1613.
Ross	Sir E. Dennison Ross, *Sir Anthony Sherley and his Persian Adventure*, Routledge, 1933.
Shirley I	Evelyn Philip Shirley, *Stemmata Shirleiana*, 2nd edn., Nichols and Sons, 1873.
Shirley II	Evelyn Philip Shirley, *The Sherley Brothers*, privately printed, 1848.
Subrahmanyam	Sanjay Subrahmanyam, *Three Ways To Be Alien*, Permanent Black, New Delhi, 2016.

Endnotes

Introduction

1. Anthony Sherley to Anthony Bacon, from Moscow, 12th Feb. 1600: Shirley II, 26.
2. Stephen Greenblatt, *Renaissance Self-Fashioning*, University of Chicago Press, 1984, 2.
3. Jean Chardin was a French traveller who spent several years in Persia.
4. The surname 'Sherley' can be spelt with a first e or an i, but for the brothers it was always 'e'.
5. Xavier A. Flores, *Le 'Peso Politico de Todo el Mundo'*, S.E.V.P.E.N., Paris, 1963, 19.
6. Dan O'Sullivan, *The Reluctant Ambassador*, Amberley Publishing, 2016.
7. Blow.
8. Penrose, 245.

Chapter 1: Sir Thomas senior

1. Evelyn Shirley thought he was born in 1563, not 1565: Shirley I, 272.
2. For the history of the Sherley family, see Evelyn Philip Shirley, *Stemmata Shirleiana*, 1873 (Shirley I).
3. *op cit*, 253.
4. *op cit*, 251.
5. Michelene White, *English Women, Religion and Textual Production, 1500-1625*, Ashgate, 2011, 61.
6. CSP Domestic, 1581-1590, 171.
7. R.C. Strong & J.A. Van Dorsten, *Leicester's Triumph*, Oxford University Press, 1964, 36-7.
8. Davies, 9.
9. *op cit*, 19-20.
10. Evelyn Philip Shirley, *The Sherley Brothers*, privately printed, 1848, 95 (Shirley II).
11. Cecil Papers, vol. VII, 142.
12. Janet Pennington, *Sir Thomas Sherley senior*, ODNB, 2016.
13. Shirley I, 256.
14. *ibid.*

Chapter 2: The brothers at war

1. Shirley I, 272; Ross, 4.
2. adapted from J. L. Motley, *History of the United Netherlands*, 1858, vol. 1, 50-51.
3. *Relation*, 3.
4. Xavier A. Flores, *Le 'Peso Politico de Todo el Mundo'*, S.E.V.P.E.N., Paris, 1963, 102-103.
5. *op cit*, 43-46; see also R. B. Wernham, *Before the Armada: The Emergence of the English Nation, 1485-1588*, Jonathan Cape, 1966, 43.
6. Richard Raiswell, *Sir Anthony Sherley*, ODNB, 2004.
7. Davies, 37.
8. Ross, 5.
9. Cecil Papers, vol. IV, 521-522.
10. Raiswell.
11. Cecil Papers, vol. V, 176, 17 April 1595.
12. CSP, Domestic, 1595-1597, 44-45.
13. Shirley II, 9-10.

Chapter 3: A privateer

1. J.A. Froude, *The Reign of Elizabeth*, 1856; Everyman edn., 1911, vol. II, 178 & 186.
2. Cecil Papers, vol. VI, 162.
3. Davies, 49-50.
4. Richard Hakluyt, *The Principal Navigations, Voyages, Traffiques and Discoveries of the English Nation, (1589);* Everyman edn., 1915, vol. VII, 213-221.
5. Penrose, 18.
6. 'The Hispanic American Historical Review', *v*ol. V, no. 2 (May 1922), 227-248.
7. Shirley II, 10.
8. Cecil Papers, vol. VII, 346.
9. CSP Domestic, 1595-7, 482.
10. Report by Sir Arthur Gorges, in Samuel Purchas, *Hakluytus Posthumus* (1625); 1907 edn., vol. XX, 92.
11. Davies, 60.

Chapter 4: To Venice

1. Shirley II, 15.
2. Cecil Papers, vol. VII, 526, 30 Dec., 1597.
3. *ibid.*
4. Parry, in Ross, 101; Manwaring, in Ross, 176.
5. Thomas Coryate, *Coryate's Crudities*. (1611); 1905 edn., 171.
6. *ibid.*
7. Neil MacGregor, *Shakespeare's Restless Worlds*, Penguin Books, 2014, 107.
8. Parry, in Ross, 101.
9. Cecil Papers, vol. VIII, 151.
10. Subrahmanyam, 93.
11. Manwaring, in Ross, 176.
12. Cecil Papers, vol. VIII, 188-189.
13. *Relation*, 4.
14. Cecil Papers, vol. VIII, 188, 2 June 1598.

Chapter 5: Sir Thomas Sherley the younger

1. CSP Domestic, 1591-94. 109, 29 Sept. 1591.
2. Davies, 63.
3. Shirley II, 13.
4. Davies, 69.
5. Shirley II, 12-13.
6. A chequin was a Turkish coin worth about eight shillings in contemporary English money.
7. Davies, 311.
8. Ross, 9 & 11.
9. Cecil Papers, vol. XIX, 173.
10. Chew, 179.

Chapter 6: The journey to Qazvīn

1. For Pinçon's authorship, see Ross, xvii-xviii.
2. For Sherley's own account see *Relation*; for those of Parry, Pinçon and Manwaring, see Ross.

3. *Relation*, 10.
4. Quotes are from Parry, in Ross, 102-3.
5. *Relation*. 5.
6. Shirley II, 17.
7. Penrose, 52.
8. Manwaring, in Ross, 179.
9. *Relation*, 8.
10. *Othello*, act 5, scene 2.
11. Manwaring, in Ross, 183-184.
12. Davies, 88.
13. *Relation*, 18.
14. *op cit*, 22.
15. *op cit*, 19.
16. Manwaring, in Ross, 189.
17. Davies, 90-91.
18. Penrose, 59.
19. Chew. 271.
20. *Relation*, 20.
21. *op cit*, 22-24.

Chapter 7: Persia before Abbas

1. Michael Axworthy, *Iran: Empire of the Mind*, Penguin Books, 2008, vii.
2. For Sufism during the time of the Safivids, see Kathryn Babayan, *Mystics, Monarchs and Messiahs*, Harvard Centre for Middle Eastern Studies, 2002, xv-xxxix.
3. Blow, 5.
4. Abbas Amanat, *Iran, A Modern History*, Yale University Press, 2017, 48.
5. Blow, 4. For how the Safavids institutionalised these rituals, see Babayan, 222-233.
6. David Blow, *Persia through Western Eyes*, Eland Publishing, 2007, 94.
7. Jerry Brotton, *The Sultan and the Queen*, Penguin Books, 2017, 52.

Chapter 8: The young Shah

1. Rumi was a 13th-century Persian poet and Sufi mystic.
2. Blow, 15-30.
3. Iskander Beg Munshi, *History of Shah Abbas the Great*, trans. Roger Savory, Westview Press, Boulder, Colorado, 1930, vol. I, 370.
4. *Don Juan,* 204.
5. The above two quotations are from Iskander Beg Munshi, vol. I, 513-514.
6. Blow, 35.

Chapter 9: The nature of Shah Abbas

1. *A Chronicle of the Carmelites*, I.B. Tauris, 2012, vol. I, 285.
2. Iskander Beg Munshi, vol. II, 892-3.
3. Blow, 173.
4. *A Chronicle of the Carmelites*, vol. I, 286.
5. Babayan, 441-443.
6. *ibid.*
7. Parry, in Ross, 107.
8. Manwaring, in Ross, 186.
9. Chew, 183.
10. Babayan, 445-6.
11. Brotton, 50.
12. Blow, 176-7.
13. *Relation*, 74.
14. Sholeh A. Quinn, *Shah 'Abbas: The King Who Refashioned Iran*, Oneworld, 2015, 62-3.
15. Babayan 350-1; Blow 42-45.
16. Manwaring, in Ross, 215.
17. Pinçon, in Ross, 160.
18. *A Chronicle of the Carmelites*, vol. I, 158.
19. Iskander Beg Munshi, vol. I, 525.
20. Manwaring, in Ross, 204-205.
21. Iskander Beg Munshi, vol. I, 529.

Chapter 10: A meeting

1. Chew, 260.
2. Ross, xx.
3. Parry, in Ross, 109.
4. Manwaring, in Ross, 201.
5. *Relation*, 64.
6. Pinçon, in Ross, 154-5; Manwaring in Ross, 206.
7. Manwaring, in Ross, 207.
8. Parry, in Ross, 118-119.
9. *Relation*, 71.
10. *op cit,* 76.
11. The following discussion takes up over twenty pages of Sherley's *Relation* (82-103).
12. *Relation*, 106.
13. *Don Juan,* 232.
14. *Relation*, 119.

Chapter 11: Travelling as an ambassador

1. *Don Juan,* 234.
2. *op cit*, 232.
3. Shirley II, 21.
4. Pinçon, in Ross, 167.
5. Parry, in Ross, 126.
6. Shirley II, 23.
7. Davies, 114-115.
8. Parry, in Ross, 131.
9. Shirley II, 23.
10. *op cit,* 26.
11. *Don Juan,* 261.
12. *op cit*, 261-262.
13. *op cit*, 336.
14. Shirley II, 28.
15. *op cit*, 30-31.
16. Chew, 273.
17. Davies, 135.
18. Ross, 47.

Chapter 12: Opinion at home

1. The following paragraphs are indebted to Jerry Brotton, *The Sultan and the Queen*, Penguin Books, 2017, especially 225-256.
2. Nabil Matar, *Turks, Moors, and Englishmen in the Age of Discovery*, Columbia University Press, 2000, 146.
3. *ibid*.
4. *op cit*, 172.
5. Brotton, 269.
6. *op cit*, 203.
7. *op cit*, 219.
8. *op cit*, 111.
9. J. L.P. Casellas, 'The Travailes of the Three English Brothers and the Textual Construction of Early Modern Identities', INTERLITT-ERARIA, 2016, p. 255.
10. Chew, 274-276.
11. Casellas, 258.

Chapter 13: Essex and honour

1. *Henry IV Part I*, Act 5, Scene 1.
2. Mervyn James, *Society, Politics and Culture*, Cambridge University Press, 1986, 325.
3. Cecil Papers, vol. X, 190, 20 June, 1600.
4. James, 423.
5. *op cit,* 455.
6. Davies, 135.
7. *ibid*.

Chapter 14: Spying – a downward trajectory

1. Shirley II, 33.
2. Subrahmanyam, 111.
3. Penrose, 120.
4. *ibid*, 120. Penrose gives a brief biography of Wilson.
5. Davies, 148.
6. Niels Steensgaard, *The Asian Trade Revolution of the Seventeenth Century*, University of Chicago Press, 1973, 263.

7. Cecil Papers, vol. XII, 322, 27 Aug. 1602.
8. *ibid.*
9. *ibid*, 6 Sept. 1602.
10. Davies, 179.
11. Ross, 57.
12. *op cit,* 64.
13. *op cit*, 67.
14. Penrose, 132.
15. Ross, 68.
16. Penrose, 140.
17. Davies, 202.
18. Shirley II, 65.
19. Penrose, 148-151 & 263-269.
20. Ross, 73.
21. Davies, 212.

Chapter 15: Abbas the Great

1. Abbas Amanant, *Iran. A Modern History*, Yale University Press, 2017, 78.
2. Michael Axworthy, *Iran, Empire of the Mind*, Penguin Books, 2008, 141.
3. Sholeh A. Quinn, *Shah Abbas: The King Who Refashioned Iran*, Oneworld, 2015, 56.
4. *op cit*, 44.
5. Blow, 218-221.
6. R. M. Savory, 'Abbas I', *Encyclopædia Iranica*; available on line at http://www.iranicaonline.org/articles/abbas-i

Chapter 16: Robert Sherley

1. Davies, 168.
2. Shirley II, 58.
3. Penrose, 179.
4. Ross, 24.
5. Shirley II, 61.
6. *op cit*, 56-59.
7. *op cit*, 72-73, 5 Feb. 1610.

8. *op cit*, 77, 30 Aug 1611.
9. Penrose, 184.
10. Shirley I, 281.
11. Nothing is known about this Henry except that he was still living in 1614, and that he died in England: Shirley I, 282.
12. *op cit*, 215-216.
13. Thomas Herbert, *Travels in Persia 1627-29*, Routledge, 1928, 125.
14. Translated by Davies, 174.

Chapter 17: *Peso Politico*

1. Shirley II, 75.
2. *ibid.*
3. Davies, 224.
4. *op cit*, 280-281.
5. *op cit*, 222.
6. *op cit*. 280.
7. *ibid.*
8. *Le 'Peso Politico de Todo el Mundo' d'Anthony Sherley*, introduced by Xavier A. Flores, S.E.V.P.E.N., Paris, 1963.
9. Niels Steensgaard, *The Asian Trade Revolution of the Seventeenth Century*, University of Chicago Press, 1973, 413 & 265.
10. Flores, introduction to *Le 'Peso Politico'*, 48.
11. The following translations into English from *Le 'Peso Politico'* are by Subrahmanyam, chapter 3.
12. Flores, 40-41.
13. *ibid*, 43-46.
14. Subrahmanyam, 128.
15. *op cit*, 121.
16. Davies, 284.
17. Subrahmanyam, 116.

Conclusion

1. Ross, 86.
2. Penrose, 244-245.
3. Davies, 285.
4. Nial Ferguson, *Civilization*, Penguin Books, 2012, xix.

Appendix I: Doubtful stories associated with the Sherleys

1. Samuel Purchas, *Hakluytus Posthumus or Purchas his Pilgrimes, contayning a History of the World in Sea Voyages and Lande Travells, by Englishmen and Others*, (1625); 1905-1907 edn., vol. X, 374.
2. Shirley II, 20.
3. R. M. Savory, 'The Sherley myth', *Iran: Journal of the British Institute of Persian Studies*, 1967, vol. 5, 73–81.
4. Manwaring, in Ross, 222.
5. Chew, 275. This manuscript diary is 'The Diary of William Smith of Abington', British Library, Sloane MS, 414.

Appendix III: The uncertainty of letters

1. Cecil Papers, vol. X, 3rd & 6th Jan. 1600.
2. Sherley II, 51.
3. *op cit*, 58.

Appendix IV: A portrait of Anthony Sherley?

1. Evelyn Shirley has Anthony Sherley being born in 1583, not 1585, which, of course, suits his argument that this portrait cannot be of Anthony.

Index

Abbas the Great, Shah of Persia,
  ix, 119.
  his inheritance, 50-55.
  his youth in Herat, and family,
    56-59.
  arrival in Qazvin and revenge
    on his enemies, 59-61.
  personal characteristics, 64-72.
  his ruthlessness, cruelty,
    70-72, 77.
  meets Sir Anthony and his
    group, 74-6.
  appoints Sir Anthony
    ambassador, 80, 84.
  receives letters from Sir
    Anthony, 110.
  economic reforms, 120-21.
  art and culture, 65-6, 122-23.
  final achievements, 124-6.
Abu Fares of Marrakesh, 113-15.
  see also Morocco,
Aleppo, 42-3, 67, 76, 95,
  centre for Persian trade, 121, 125.
Ali Beg, Hussein, joint
  ambassador with Sir Anthony,
  83-6, 89-90, 97.
Allaverdi Khan, Abbas's leading
  general, 54, 61.
  his support for Sir Anthony,
    77-8.

Arundel, Anne Howard, Countess
  of, 3.
Astrology, 70.

Bacon, Anthony, secretary to
  Essex, 85.
Baghdad:
  a low point in Sir Anthony's
    journey to Persia, 45-7.
  lost to the Ottomans during
    Tamasp's reign, 53.
  recaptured by Abbas, 125.

Cecil, Sir Robert (later Lord
  Salisbury), 104.
  receives letters from the
    Sherleys, 7, 14, 31, 40, 87.
    110, 115, 130.
  helps Sir Anthony join the
    Islands Voyage, 21.
  invests in a voyage by
    Sir Thomas Sherley,
    junior, 33.
  investigates Sir Thomas,
    junior, after his return from
    Turkey, 38.
  his interest in Robert Sherley's
    scheme, 131.
  his agents, 110, 155.
  his death, 132.

Chaloner, Sir Thomas, viii-ix, 29.
Chaldiran, battle of, 51-2, 126.
Clark, William, merchant in Aleppo, 43, 45.
Clement VIII, Pope:
   meets Sir Anthony and Ali Beg, 80.
Coffee and coffee houses, 66-7.
Cornwallis, Sir Charles, English ambassador in Madrid, 116.
Corrai, Angelo, Sir Anthony's interpreter, 28, 42, 73, 80.
Coulthurst, Richard, leading British merchant in Aleppo. 42, 45.

Day, John, playwright:
   co-author of *The Travailes of the Three English Brothers*, 97-100.
Don Juan, Persian who converted to Christianity, 82, 85-6.
Drake, Sir Francis:
returns from circumnavigating the world, 16.
Dudley, Robert, Leicester's illegitimate son, 31-2, 34.

East India Company, 119, 124, 131, 134,
Elizabeth, Queen of England, 1, 3, 30, 80, 87-8, 93.
   her anger over Leicester's governorship of the Netherlands, 5.
   sends an army to France in 1591, 13.
   anger over Sir Anthony's knighthood, 13-14.
   criticises Essex for failure of Islands Voyage, 22.
Essex, Robert Devereux, Earl of, viii, 1, 30.
   relationship with Elizabeth, 102-3.
   with Sir Anthony, 103.
   leads cavalry at Zutphen, 10-11, 102.
   expedition to Cadiz, 104.
   the Islands Voyage, 21-2.
   in Ireland, 105-6.
   Sir Anthony's letter of support to him, 88.
   fall from power and execution, 105-6.
see also Honour

Ferdinand, Grand Duke of Tuscany, 34.
Ferrara project, 1, 25-6, 89, 104.

Gunpowder, its use in Persia, 51, 119-20, 128, 149-50.
Godunov, Boris, Czar of Russia:
   retains Sir Anthony in Moscow, 84-5.

Harborne, William, first English ambassador in Constantinople, 94-5.
Hayder Beg, Shah Abbas's vizier, 78-9.
Henry IV of France, 12-15, 80. 103. 109.

Index

Hamza, Prince, brother of Shah Abbas, 59, 63.
Honour, 30.
   Essex's culture of honour and its decline, 11, 101-8.
   Sir Anthony's place in Essex's honour culture, 14.
   'that unseen thing called honour', 85.
   a novel concept for Persians, 99.
   Sir Anthony redefines his own honour, 146.
Hormuz, Portuguese trading base, 76, 84, 119, 130.
   captured from Portuguese, 124-5.

Isfahan, 67, 84.
   Persian capital moved there, 121,
   Sir Anthony arrives there, 77.
   city's growth under Abbas, 121-3.
Islands Voyage, 17, 21-2, 104.
Ismail I, Shah of Persia, 50-53, 55, 62-3, 76.
Ismail II, 57-8, 63.

James VI and I, King of Scotland and England, 82, 109, 116.
   employs Sir Anthony in Morocco, 113.
   meets Robert Sherley (twice), 131, 133.
   his death, 134.
Jenkinson, Anthony, Muscovy Company merchant, 54-5, 68.

Kemp, Will, actor, 98, 150.
Kydman, William:
   harshly treated by Sir Anthony *on* their journey to Persia, 44-5.

Leicester, Robert Dudley, Earl of, 3, 11.
   in the Netherlands, 4-6, 102.
   retirement and death, 12.
Leghorn (now Livorno), port in Tuscany, 34-5.
Lello, Henry, English ambassador at Constantinople:
   writes to Robert Cecil on Sir Anthony's behalf, 40.
   tries to help Sir Thomas, junior, a prisoner of the Turks, 37.
   warned about Sir Anthony by Queen Elizabeth, 87.
Letters of Marque, 17, 32.
Levant Company, 95, 131, 133.

Mahd-e Oliva, mother of Shah Abbas, 56, 58-9, 63.
Manwaring, George, travelled with Sir Anthony Sherley, 39, 82, 96.
   excerpts from his diary, 42-4, 67, 70, 149-50.
Mary, Queen of Scots:
   her alleged message to the Duke of Parma, 12, 142.
Melo, Nicholas de, friar who accompanied Sir Anthony to Moscow, 81, 84-5.

Moghul emperors, 119, 123-5, 132.
   their loss of Kandahar to Abbas, 125.
Mohammad Aga, Turkish ambassador to Shah Abbas, 79-80.
Mohammad Khodabanda, father of Shah Abbas, 56-60, 63.
Morocco, 91, 94.
   Sir Anthony's Moroccan project, 113-15.

Nixon, Anthony, pamphleteer, 34-6, 94-8, 115.
Norris, Sir John, 13, 103.

Oglander, Sir John:
   supports Sir Thomas Sherley, junior, during his retirement, 38.
Olivares, Duke of:
   and *Peso Politico*, 139, 142-4.
Ottomans, 93, 100. 119-20, 142.
   see also Turkey.
Othello, 42, 92.

Pagliarini, Giovanni, Sir Anthony's secretary, 109, 116-17.
Parma, Alexander Farnese, Duke of, 3-4, 10.
   said to have received a message from Mary, Queen of Scots, 12, 142.
Parry, William, travelled with Sir Anthony, 67, 74, 76, 82.
   leaves the group for England, 87-8.
   his diary published, 96.

Philip II of Spain, 138.
Philip III of Spain, 108, 110, 113, 138.
   makes Sir Anthony an admiral, 116,
   his reception of Robert Sherley, 130.
Pinçon, Abel, travelled with Sir Anthony Sherley, 39, 74, 82.
   from his diary, 70-1, 83.
Potso, Hugo de, Portuguese merchant:
   enemy of Sir Anthony, 39, 41, 43.
Powell, Thomas, 'gunner', 128-9, 132.

Qizilbash tribes,
   devotion to their Sufi leaders, 59.
   main component of Safavid forces, 62.
   their resentment of female leaders, 58.
   new non-tribal forces created, 53-4.
   remain the backbone of the army under Abbas, 120.

'Raleigh, Sir Walter:
   on Islands Voyage, 21-22.
   opposes Essex, 104.
   search for El Dorado, 138.
Rudolf II, Emperor, 80, 84, 88, 109, 112.
   sends Sir Anthony to Morocco, 113.
   cedes authority to his brother, Mathias, 115.
   makes Sir Anthony a count, 117.

Index

Safavid dynasty, 49-50, 53, 124, 126.
Sherley family, 2, 63.
  Anne (née Kempe), wife of Sir Thomas, senior, 2, 98.
  Sir Anthony, viii-x.
    at war in the Netherlands, 9-12
    and in France, 12-13, 103.
    his attachment to the Earl of Essex, 11-12.
    knighted by Henry IV, 13.
    marriage to Frances Vernon. 14-15.
    as privateer, 16-21.
    joins the Islands Voyage, 21-22.
    sets out for Ferrara, 1 (*see also* Ferrara project).
    in Venice, 25-30.
    arrives in Qazvin, 74-5.
    appointed ambassador, 80.
    hears of Essex's execution, 89.
    meets Will Kemp, 98.
    interrogation, and expulsion from Venice, 111-13.
    sent to Morocco (*see also* Abu Fares, Morocco), 113.
    as an admiral working for Spain, 116-18.
    retires to Granada, 137-38.
    his *Relation of his travels*, 39, 41, 73.
    his reputation in England, 95-100.
    historians' views about him, 146-47.
    portraits of him, 156-57.
    his death, 144-45.
  Diego (Anthony's son), 15, 144, 147.
  Frances (née Vavasour), Sir Thomas, junior's first wife, 31, 38.
  Henry (Robert's son), 131-2.
  Judith (née Taylor), Sir Thomas, junior's second wife, 38.
  Robert
    joins Sir Anthony's group in Venice, 30.
    hits a ship captain, 40.
    joins in dialogues with Persians, 77, 79.
    his character compared with Sir Anthony's, 127-30.
    his marriage, and conversion to the Catholic faith, 129.
    his correspondence with Sir Anthony, 128-29, 155.
    first journey to Europe as ambassador, 129-132.
    meets Sir Anthony in Madrid, 118, 137.
    takes Anthony's *Relation* to England, 73.
    his son, 96.
    second journey as ambassador, 133-35.
    death and epitaph, 135-6.
  Teresia, wife of Robert, 120, 130, 132, 136.
  Sir Thomas, senior:
    at Wiston, 2-3.

in the Netherlands, 4-7.
finances Sir Anthony's
  privateering voyage, 17.
his debts to the Crown,
  7, 32.
denies consenting
  to Sir Anthony's
  marriage, 16.
his anger at Sir Thomas,
  junior's marriage, 31.
suggests the idea
  of baronets to
  King James I, 7-8.
his letters seized by Cecil's
  agents, 155.
his death and effigy, 8, 130.
Sir Thomas, junior:
  as a captain in the
    Netherlands, 9-10.
  knighted in Ireland, 10.
  marriage to Frances
    Vavasour, 31.
  as a privateer, 32-35.
  prisoner of the
    Turks, 35-37.
  his *Discourse on the Turks*,
    31-3, 91-2, 95.
Shi'ism, official religion of
  Safavid Persia, 52-3, 67-9.
Sidney, Sir Philip, 102.
Skinner, John, merchant who
  invested in Sir Thomas,
  junior's voyages, 32.
Speciero, Victorio, who saved Sir
  Anthony Sherley from disaster
  in Baghdad, 43, 46-7.

Steyning, pocket borough
  controlled by the Sherleys, 2, 7.
Sufism, 49-52.
  see also Ismail I.
Surtees, Rev. Scott, 98-9, 150-51.

Tahmasp, Shah of Persia, 53-55,
  57, 62-3, 68, 119,
  see also Safavid dynasty,
    Shi'ism.
Townsend, Aurelian, Cecil's agent
  in Venice, 110.
Turkey, 76-80, 91, 96, 100, 110-12.
  trade with England, 131.
  'more powerful than Persia', 140.
  see also Ottomans.

Uzbeks, 53, 61-2,
  defeated by Abbas, 72, 74, 76,
    119, 121.

Vere, Sir Francis:
  his letter to Sir Anthony, 82-3.

Willoughby, Bertie, Lord, 6, 103.
Wilson, Thomas, Cecil's agent in
  Venice, 110-11.
Wiston, family home of the
  Sherleys, 2-3, 8, 130, 132.
Wotton, Sir Henry, diplomat, 89.

Zutphen, skirmish at, 10-11.
  19, 102.
Zwolle:
  Sir Thomas Sherley, junior, as
    governor. 10.